EDWARD SAID
CONTINUING THE CONVERSATION

EDWARD SAID

CONTINUING THE CONVERSATION

EDITED BY

HOMI BHABHA AND W.J.T. MITCHELL

THE UNIVERSITY OF CHICAGO PRESS

CHICAGO AND LONDON

The University of Chicago Press, Chicago 60637
The University of Chicago Press, Ltd., London
09 08 07 06 05   5 4 3 2 1

Library of Congress Cataloging-in-Publication Data
Edward Said : continuing the conversation / Edward Said ; edited by Homi
Bhabha and W.J.T. Mitchell.
    p. cm.
    ISBN 0-226-53201-1 (cloth : alk. paper) — ISBN 0-226-53203-8 (pbk.)
    1. Said, Edward W. 2. Intellectuals—United States. 3. Criticism. I. Title:
Continuing the coversation. II. Said, Edward W. III. Bhabha, Homi K., 1949–
IV. Mitchell, W. J. Thomas, 1942–
CB18.S25E385 2005
801′.95′092—dc22   2005000626

Edward Said: Continuing the Conversation
Edited by Homi Bhabha and W. J. T. Mitchell

On the cover: Photo courtesy of Mariam Said.

Edward Said: Continuing the Conversation

W. J. T. Mitchell *?*

*what is an
"actuint intellectual"
·* *is*

On the morning after Edward Said's death, Homi Bhabha and I had a phone conversation about the ways in which *Critical Inquiry* might best respond to this tragic and untimely event. The pace of a scholarly journal does not make for timely utterances of grief, and Edward's many friends, colleagues, former students, and readers were casting about for a way to honor his legacy as an activist intellectual. We discussed the possibility of assembling a special issue on Edward's work but found ourselves baffled by the enormous range of choices. Should we stress his literary, humanistic writing and teaching? His musical criticism and his work as a musical activist in collaboration with Daniel Barenboim? His role as a cultural theorist, from his early assessments of French theory in *Beginnings* to his latest reflections on postcolonial theory? Or should we stress his importance as a political commentator, an engaged intellectual who emerged as the most eloquent spokesman for (and acerbic critic of) the Palestinian movement in the last quarter century? So many topics! So little certainty about what was needed *right now*.

We settled, finally, on no topic at all, but simply on a bit of utopian wish fulfilment. We decided to do the impossible and ask a range of intellectuals, all of them longtime friends and collaborators, to *continue the conversation* with Edward where they had left off, to take up the issues that seemed unresolved or in need of fuller elaboration. We did not want to predict where this might take us, whether it would take the form of rigorous elaborations on certain ideas in Edward's writing, applications of his thought to new problems, or more personal recollections of the undescribable electricity that made conversation with Edward so intense and memorable. In what follows, you will find all these strategies and more. Our aim has been not

to compartmentalize Said's work in terms of disciplinary or topical boundaries; not to provide "assessments" of his positions on a variety of issues
from some position of imaginary objectivity; and not to mobilize his work
on behalf of any particular poltical or intellectual agenda. We have sought
rather to trace the living filaments of Said's thought as they were woven into
the presence of his voice in his writing and speaking, his public persona and
his private self. All of our contributors were in more or less constant dialogue with Said, either in private or public, and all of them are known for
their prowess in the give and take of debate. We thought it would be an
interesting challenge for them, first, to imagine (and remember) the ca-
dences of Edward's conversation; second, to project those into the present
and into possible futures; and, third, to see where this would take us, what
critical possibilities are opened up by this impossible task.

The only way I know to test an assignment of this sort is to prescribe it
for oneself, which is what I did in the days immediately following Edward's
death. I took the idea (I believe it was Homi's) of continuing the conversation and wrote the following pages, which will serve as a preface to this
collection.[1] My more sober second thoughts appear within the collection
itself.

Any guise of critical neutrality or objectivity drops away when it comes
to the death (and life) of Edward Said. Edward was a profound influence
on *Critical Inquiry,* the scholarly journal I have edited for the last twenty-
five years, a frequent contributor, and a crucial member of our advisory
board. He was one of the greatest scholar-critics of his generation, opening
up entire new fields of thought and research for thousands of people in and
out of the academic world. But he was also my dear, cherished friend for
twenty-two years and was to me both an inimitable exemplar of the highest
calling of the intellectual life and something like a teasing, needling older
brother—smarter, better looking, better dressed, more sophisticated, always out ahead somewhere on horizons that for me were just coming into
view. He opened innumerable doors and windows for me and seemed to
regard me as something of a reclamation project—a rude American west-
erner badly in need of guidance and reeducation, especially in matters of
clothing. Our usual ritual upon meeting after some time apart was for him

---

1. An earlier version of these pages appeared in the *Chronicle of Higher Education* and
subsequently in the editorial notes to the winter 2004 issue of *Critical Inquiry.*

W. J. T. MITCHELL is the Gaylord Donnelley Distinguished Service Professor
of English and art history at the University of Chicago and editor of *Critical
Inquiry.* His latest book, *What Do Pictures Want?* will appear in 2005.

to look me up and down and pass withering judgments on the condition of my shoes and to berate my obstinate reluctance to engage a proper tailor.

I have no idea how many hours we spent talking on the phone or face-to-face over meals during the last twenty years. Since our first meeting at the 1981 *Critical Inquiry* conference on "The Politics of Interpretation" (where he delivered his memorable paper on "Opponents, Audiences, Constituencies, and Community"), our conversation was rarely interrupted for more than a month or two. We shared secrets and passions, surprises and standing jokes, gossip and grievances, and marathon tennis matches on Columbia University's clay courts. We argued constantly—over literary theory, new critical movements, postmodernism, deconstruction, politics, editorial decisions, and questions of taste. His characteristic strategy was to reduce me to silence and then to turn the debate around and express some doubt about what he had been arguing and to urge me to put up a better fight, like a boxer carrying his opponent for an extra round or two. This was, I feel, part of his larger critical strategy of cutting against the grain, questioning received ideas (including his own), and treating the critical encounter, not as a matter of system or position, but of dialogic transformation. We shared a love for William Blake and especially for certain of his "Proverbs of Hell": "Opposition Is True Friendship"; "Without Contraries Is No Progression."

Others can write with greater authority on Said's intellectual achievements as a scholar of music, literature, and the arts, and as a spokesman for the Palestinians. No one, I think, can quite grasp the totality of his ambitions—his voracious reading in history and politics, in the literatures of Europe, the Americas, and the Middle East. For me, the characteristic gesture of both his cultural and political writing (which, despite his claim to lead "two lives," always seemed to me all of a piece) was the *turn* from the straight, predictable path, the reversal of field, the interrupted itinerary. So that, having by many accounts founded the entire field of what is called postcolonial studies, he immediately set about to critique it, to question its emergent complacencies and received ideas. His role as spokesman for Palestine involved similar turns and complexities. He often said that he wanted to help bring a Palestinian state into existence so that then he could play his proper role as critic and attack it. His most profound reflection on the Palestinian people is, in my view, *After the Last Sky*, a book-length essay written in collaboration with the great Swiss photographer Jean Mohr. This book took a double risk, engaging with a visual art form (a medium that Said often confessed put him into a "panic") and with the interior, private lives of an oppressed people whose lives are and were in many ways quite alien to the cosmopolitan and rather aristocratic life that Edward enjoyed. The result is a marvelous, many-layered reflection on images of the Palestinians, the stereotypes circulated about them, but also *by* them; their fantasies and fixations, virtues and vices. The book is, of course, an impassioned plea for international recognition of the justice of Palestinian claims and a polemic against the hideous occupation and dispossession they have suffered for half a century. But, much more importantly, it is a mirror *for* the Palestinians, a critical reflection on their political mistakes, their cultural shortcomings. Above all, it is a confession of Said's own ambiguous relation to his people, which is nothing like that of a spokesman in the usual sense—that is, a mouthpiece for power. Edward was a spokesman in the way the Jewish prophets spoke for and to Israel: a chiding, challenging voice, sometimes in the wilderness, sometimes in the opera house or symphony hall, sometimes at the movies or in the preface to a book of poems or a graphic documentary, and sometimes in the academic lecture theater, always speaking the unwelcome truth to power.

For me, the voice of these public occasions was inseparable from the avuncular, teasing figure so often found at the head of the dinner table of Rashid Khalidi, the eminent Palestinian historian and a longtime friend and colleague at the University of Chicago. There the banter with friends and relatives—black and white, Jew and Arab, Irish and English and Indian—over Mona Khalidi's cooking made instantaneous transitions from the personal to the political, the academic to the public sphere. His voice on the telephone, no matter how racked with illness in the last couple of years, could, without a hitch, transform itself into the voice heard so often on PBS or BBC—an eloquent, insistent intelligence grounded in depths of learning and feeling and leavened by a wicked sense of humor and passionate indignation. Walking and talking with Edward were one and the same thing: a headlong, breathless, long-legged conversation, heedless of curbs, interrupted without warning by full stops. I would suddenly find myself walking alone, turning back toward his look of astonishment, or grabbed by the arm and pulled up short: "But, dear boy, you cannot be serious!" Or, "No! *Really!?* Just as I always suspected!" Neither the low places of academic politics nor the high places of global strategizing were spared the lash of his wit and the exercise of his intelligence. No ally, no matter how close, was above criticism; no opponent exempt from the verbal cruelty of which he was a master.

Said was, it should be remembered, a polemicist, a literary warrior in the tradition of Jonathan Swift. His wicked humor and teasing in private life became unbridled satire on the public page. He was often angry at *Critical Inquiry* (and at me) for publishing articles that were critical of him, and he once denounced a hapless opponent in our "Critical Response" section as a fictitious person, a fraudulent assemblage of ideological cliches. He was an angry young man, an angry middle-aged man, and he was learning how to play the brilliant curmudgeon, endlessly chastising his would-be followers and younger colleagues for being slaves of fashion and for writing barbarous, jargon-ridden prose. And of course he inspired anger, hatred, resentment, envy in others. He was constantly being accused of lacking balance in his political writings, failing to condemn Palestinian terrorism as frequently and vehemently as he attacked Israel's state terrorism—as if any polemicist worthy of the name has ever been known for *balance,* as if there were some moral calculus that requires every condemnation of the violence of the strong to be balanced by an equal-time condemnation of the resistance of the weak.

Edward's public appearances were plagued by death threats that he dismissed (along with his cancer) as an annoying distraction and (even worse) by questioners who wanted to lure him into anti-Semitic comments or to characterize his criticisms of Israel as expressions of anti-Semitism. (This canard has now been institutionalized by a nationwide campaign to hurl accusations of racism at intellectuals who question Israeli policies in any way; in this sense, we have all become Edward Saids.) Edward never wavered in his resistance to the seductions of hate speech and hateful thinking in public or private. In his conversation one could sense the presence of numerous Jewish interlocutors, of the intimate connectness of Palestinian and Jewish cultures and histories, of the feeling for peoples linked by a common tragic destiny, as if the Palestinians could be thought of as the Jews of the Jews. Although he did not speak Hebrew, he liked to quote the Palestinian poet Mahmoud Darwish, who talks of making love in the Hebrew language he had learned as a child.

We spent a week together in the West Bank and Israel in the fall of 1998 on the occasion of a remarkable international conference at Birzeit University. The conference, "Landscape Perspectives on Palestine," was the most profoundly affecting academic gathering I have ever attended. (The proceedings were later published as *The Landscape of Palestine: Equivocal Poetry* in 1999). With participants from every corner of the globe, every discipline of the humanities and social sciences, mixing Israeli and Palestinian intellectuals, it now seems like a distant, utopian moment of hope for peace in the Middle East. A new generation seemed poised to take over from the old warriors, Arafat and Sharon, ready to move into a time (which now seems unimaginable) of reconciliation and mutual discovery. Edward, the late Ibrahim Abu-Lughod, and I travelled by car with relative ease from Ramallah to Jerusalem to Jaffa, visiting childhood places, looking for "disappeared" Palestinian villages and neighborhoods, getting lost in the Orthodox Jewish section of Jerusalem, and swimming in the Mediterranean.

Edward, always a powerful swimmer, quickly left us behind in the shallows and swam far out into the sea until his head was just a dot, appearing and disappearing in the swells. He has swum out too far for us to follow now. But the ebb and flow of his conversation continues and will continue in the criticism, the politics, the culture, and the evolution of human thought to come.

Adagio

Homi Bhabha

On that day in the fall of 2003 when Edward Said lost his long struggle against all the odds, I remember thinking that we would never hear *that* voice again. His writings were indestructible, his presence memorable, but the fire and fragility of his voice—the ground note of the "individual particular" from which all human narration begins—[1] would be impossible to preserve for another conversation on literature, music, illness, and common friends. Ours was a friendship of infrequent meetings supplemented by telephone conversations, and it was the silencing of his voice that would mark his death. The large gathering of friends, colleagues, and admirers who met at Riverside Church to mourn Edward Said's passing bore testimony to a powerful, public voice that would be long remembered. But this was also the occasion on which his son, Wadie Said, spoke with love, courage, and a touch of childlike incredulity at his father's ability to ever get any work done because he was always on the telephone. *Edward Said: Continuing the Conversation* is an attempt to capture the telephonic timbre in his life and work. Our call to our contributors (the fellowship of the phone!) encouraged them to write with the telephone ringing in their ears waiting to be answered rather than the death knell of disconnection and silence. Speak to Edward, we said, in the spirit of a conversation interrupted, a call on hold, a letter waiting for a reply, a question hanging in the air. Our writers have responded with an imaginative expectancy, and they have turned to his work with questions, reflections, and interventions that have continued the conversation with a compelling candor. You can almost see Edward move

---

1. Edward W. Said, *Humanism and Democratic Criticism* (New York, 2004), p. 80; hereafter abbreviated *HDC*.

ever so slightly forward to reply, his eyes lit by a friendly but guarded half-shy smile, his long fingers working busily through the argument, making his point, beating the air to rid us of some fond illusion. "What, *what?*" he would say, his voice rising slightly, incredulous and unshakable, "you can't really be serious."

A sudden turn in Said's voice, heard in a *Diacritics* interview when I was a graduate student at Oxford, set off a bell that summoned me to reflect on my own conflicted beginnings. The turn comes in the midst of a discussion of the work of Harold Bloom, when Said admits to performing "a kind of acrobatics" between parallel lives, as avant-garde critic and Palestinian exile.

> My whole background in the Middle East, my frequent and sometimes protracted visits there, my political involvement: all this exists in a to-tally different box from the one out of which I pop as a literary critic, professor, etc. . . . I am as aware as anyone that the ivory-tower concerns of technical criticism—I use the phrase because it is very useful as a way of setting off what I and the others we've mentioned do from the non-theoretical, non-philosophically based criticism normally found in aca-demic departments of literature—are very far removed from the world of politics, power, domination, and struggle. But there are links between the two worlds which I for one am beginning to exploit in my own work.[2]

The acrobat attempts to achieve a balance between the two worlds, and he returns to the subject of Bloom in an expansive and generous mood: "whatever his political beliefs (Republican or Democratic, Marxist or anti-Marxist) he's hit on something I find absolutely true: that human activity . . . cannot take place without power relationships of the sort he talks about in poetry."[3] I immediately identified with the precariousness of Said's ac-robatics and learnt much from his ability to be otherwise engaged, both politically and philosophically, and yet to be capable of a critical assessment that was free and fair. Said's reflections on the complexities of a working life—the twists and turns between theoretical interests and social commit-

---

2. Said, "Beginnings," interview with *Diacritics*, in *Power, Politics, and Culture: Interviews with Edward W. Said*, ed. Guari Viswanathan (New York, 2001), p. 14.
   3. Ibid., p. 15.

HOMI BHABHA is Anne F. Rothenberg Professor of English and American Literature at Harvard University, Distinguished Visiting Professor, University College, London, and a Radcliffe Institute for Advanced Study Fellow for 2004–5. His two forthcoming books are entitled *A Measure of Dwelling* and *The Right to Narrate*.

ments—were remarkably timely because I was involved in a balancing act of my own.

I was writing on V. S. Naipaul and found myself in something of a quandary. His political opinions on the history of the Third World can be provocative and offensive, even as his insights upon the lifeworld of postcolonial societies are subtle, sharp, surprising. It would have been easy to condemn the former and applaud the latter; and I could have argued, as critics often do, that artists and writers are most creative when they are most contradictory and that literary language works best when it embraces the arts of agonism and ambiguity. My task, however, was tougher than that because the imaginative value of Naipaul's writing lies in its peculiar perversity. His narratives embody their negative energies and prejudicial perspectives with a ferocious passion that is, at once, dogmatic and diagnostic. The reader is given unusual insights into the psychic and affective structures that inform the politics of everyday life as it is lived in the midst of the protocols of colonial power and its contest of cultures. You might find many of Naipaul's ideological positions to be morally and politically objectionable, as I do and Said certainly did; and you may be convinced that they need to be vigorously resisted and opposed, as Said famously did, and I have, too; but contestation and refutation, Said persuasively argues, should be grounded in a philological responsibility that extends to one's affiliates and to one's adversaries. Both aspects of the philological process—reception and resistance—are practices of a skeptical *"para-doxical mode of thought"* that have to risk offending "right-minded people on the two sides" if they are to achieve a humanistic perspective that is both worldly and oppositional (*HDC*, p. 83).

In his posthumously published *Humanism and Democratic Criticism,* Said argues powerfully for a philological practice at the very heart of the project of humanism:

> What I have been calling philological, that is, a detailed, patient scrutiny of and a lifelong attentiveness to the words and rhetorics by which language is used by human beings who exist in history . . . . Thus a close reading of a literary text—a novel, poem, essay, or drama, say—in effect will gradually locate the text in its time as part of a whole network of relationships whose outlines and influence play an informing role *in* the text. And I think it is important to say that for the humanist, the act of reading is the act therefore of first putting oneself in the position of the author, for whom writing is a series of decisions and choices expressed in words. [*HDC*, pp. 61–62]

The philological imperative is a curious, paradoxical thing: an exercise in "close reading" effected through critical distance; an act of interpretation that inhabits the locality of the text (its times, decisions, choices) by wandering through the outlying networks of *les routes peripheriques;* and the process of putting yourself *in the place of* the author, which is a form of affiliation but also a partial substitution and subversion of authorial sovereignty in favor of the critic's revisionary practice. This philological commitment leads to an ironic and agonistic mode of humanistic resistance—a "technique of trouble," Said calls it—echoing R. P. Blackmur's definition of modernism. It is politically progressive *and* temporally recursive; historically contextual *because* it is aesthetically contrapuntal; secular and worldly, its feet on the ground, *despite* its engagement with the provisionality of the present, with "history as an agonistic process still being made" (*HDC*, p. 25). Such paradoxical forms of thought and belief yield the enigmatic burden of the critical humanist's view of emancipation: a song of freedom sung even as the shadows fall across our belief in human survival:

> Humanism, I think, is the means, perhaps the consciousness we have for providing that kind of finally antinomian or oppositional analysis between the space of words and their various origins and deployments in physical and social place, from text to actualized site of either appropriation or resistance, to transmission, to reading and interpretation, from private to public, from silence to explication and utterance, and back again, as we encounter our own silence and mortality—all of it occurring in the world, on the ground of daily life and history and hopes, and the search for knowledge and justice, and then perhaps also for liberation. [*HDC*, p. 83]

In this passage, as in so many others, Said speaks in a polyphonic voice weaving together his various subjects with a fugal virtuosity. The antinomian attitude references the radical culture of American humanism; oppositional analyses conceived of in spatial metaphors bring the occupied lands and displaced people of Palestine to the fore; and the quest for knowledge and justice joined in the face of silence and mortality encourages a more general reflection on the unending struggle between human survival and social sovereignty. I cannot read a line of Said's work without being reminded of the salience he gives to the Palestinian situation; and I do not encounter a word of his writings without being made aware of his concern for the human condition. What do we know, nonetheless, of the emergent, recurrent space *between* the realm of words and field of social action occupied by the humanist consciousness and its philological criticism? How do we describe the circuit of experience through which utterance is actualized and resistance achieved before both *turn back again* to silence and mortality?

These are not simply cyclical movements from life to death or from human history to mute nature; silence and mortality, as I read them, are also signs of social death, sites of oppression and exclusion, traces of the denial of human rights, memorials to those willed lapses of memory that bury the past of displaced and colonized peoples. Said's humanism is not simply a contribution to philological hermeneutics and the philosophy of history; it is also a fruitful reflection on the place of narrative in the practices of everyday life. *After the Last Sky,* Said's poignant and polyphonic portrait of "scene[s] of regular life inside Palestine *[min dakhil Filastin],*"[4] is a meditation on the ethical and political rights that must be restored to subject peoples in order to enable them to narrate their authoritative histories. Said poses questions concerning the role of narrative in the struggle for equitable representation while plotting the displaced lives of the Palestinian peoples (now further fragmented by the Wall and overrun by new settlements) across the unsettled borders of diverse *genres*—testimonies, conversations, ethnographies, photographs, memoirs. Philological humanism harbors an interest in the idea of narration as part of its commitment to close reading and revisionary interpretation; but that pedagogical perspective is surpassed by the commitment of "humanistic resistance" (Said's term) to what appears to be the performative function of narration in "maintaining rather than resolving the tension between the aesthetic and the national, using the former to challenge, reexamine and resist the latter in those slow but rational modes of reception and understanding which is the humanist's way" (*HDC*, p. 78). Why must the narrative of resistance be "slow"?

In an earlier discussion of resistance Said inveighs against the media culture of headlines, sound bites, and telegraphic forms whose rapidity renders the world one-dimensional and homogeneous. Humanist critique must oppose such eye-catching, mind-numbing institutions of instantaneity and adopt narrative forms that are longer and slower, "longer essays, longer periods of reflection" (*HDC*, p. 73). But there is, in my view, more to be said about the uses of slow reflection for humanist practice than its association with the rational would lead us to believe. Slowness is a deliberative measure of ethical and political reflection that maintains tension rather than resolves it; it is a temporal register that regulates the narrative movement through which (in negotiating the unresolved tension between the aesthetic and the national) we make "those connections that allow us to see part and whole, that is the main thing: what to connect with, how, and how not?" (*HDC*, p. 78). In making visible the complex and conflictual relations of part and whole—overdetermination, liminality, translation, displacement, minori-

---

4. Said, *After the Last Sky: Palestinian Lives* (New York, 1999), p. 76; hereafter abbreviated *A*.

tization, domination—slowness articulates the movement that exists *between* the space of words and the social world, and it strengthens our resolve to make difficult and deliberate choices relating to knowledge and justice— "how, and how not?"—in the face of contingency, silence, and mortality.

The slow narrative of humanistic critique creates opportunities for oppositional writing—the resistance of the part to the hegemonic whole—in the process of constructing subaltern or antinomian solidarities: whom to connect with? how do I form my chain of witnesses, my interdependent systems of support that enable "the practice of identities other than those given by the flag or the national war of the moment" (*HDC*, p. 80)? Said's response to such questions would be twofold. He would suggest, perhaps, that the importance of keeping alive the tension between part and whole is crucial to his own Adorno-inspired political phenomenology of the exile— bearer of oppositional analyses and maker of antinomian alliances. In the realm of the new humanistic learning this slow tension of open questions and emerging fields—located between partial realms and holistic cultures—would promote a minoritarian curriculum based on what Said describes in an interview as "massive transversals of one realm into another; . . . . the study of . . . integrations and interdependence [that is, "emergent transnational forces like Islam"] versus studies dominated by nationalities and national traditions."[5] He recommends the study of refugee societies in order to unsettle the paradigmatic stability of cultural institutions that underpin the traditional assumptions of the social sciences; and he resists the "separate essentialization" of national or cultural ideal-types—*the* Jew, *the* Indian, *the* French—because such "universals" represent the imperial legacy "by which a dominant culture eliminated the impurities and hybrids that make up all cultures."[6] Salman Rushdie is enthusiastically welcomed into the humanistic fold for having performed a transformative act of postcolonial magic by "introduc[ing] a particular kind of hybrid experience into English."[7] And Said admires García Márquez and Rushdie for their interest in issues of exile, immigration, and the crossing of boundaries and considers the "whole notion of a hybrid text" as practiced by them to be "one of the major contributions of late-twentieth-century culture."[8]

The slow pace of critical reflection resists processes of totalization—an-

5. Said, "Criticism, Culture, and Performance," interview with Bonnie Marranca, Marc Robinson, and Una Chaudhuri, *Power, Politics, and Culture*, p. 115.

6. Said, *Musical Elaborations* (New York, 1991), p. 52; hereafter abbreviated *ME*.

7. Said, "The Road Less Traveled," interview with Nirmala Lakshman, *Power, Politics, and Culture*, p. 416.

8. Said, "Criticism and the Art of Politics," interview with Jennifer Wicke and Michael Sprinker, *Power, Politics, and Culture*, p. 148.

alytic, aesthetic, or political—because they are prone to making "transitionless leaps" into realms of transcendental value, and such claims must be severely scrutinized (*HDC*, p. 80). The secular narrative of slowness and revisionary repetition has a remarkable capacity for enduring and enunciating unsettled states of transition, moments when history seems to be in a hiatus, times at which the humanist's faith hesitates or loses hope. In repeatedly asking the question of the part from the minoritarian perspective, posing that slow question of articulation and affiliation—"what to connect with, how, and how not?"—both enlarges and transgresses the civil society of the nation by confronting its self-regarding and self-enclosing sovereignty with the right to settlement of the unnamed and the undocumented:

> Always and constantly the undocumented turbulence of unsettled and unhoused exiles, immigrants, itinerant or captive populations for whom no document, no adequate expression yet exists to take account of what they go through . . . . Humanism, I strongly believe, must excavate the silences, the world of memory, of itinerant, barely surviving groups, the places of exclusion and invisibility, the kind of testimony that doesn't make it onto the reports. [*HDC*, p. 81]

When you are so severely out of place, your recovery may also seem somewhat slow, out of time, bit by bit, part upon part. And at that point, in the paradoxical style of humanist thinking, you are forced to ask: Who sets the pace of my historical recovery of land, rights, and respect? are these partial moments, and movements, a kind of regrouping of forces, or do they yield to a dominating strategy of divide and rule?

Said asks himself questions like these in the mid-1980s, and his response to them is mixed. Since 1967 there has been a growth of "smaller, more varied configurations," institutions of Palestinian civil society committed to the ideal of *sumud* (both the principles of and the group of Palestinians willing to stay in the Occupied Territories, being steadfast in their desire to stay on against the odds) that disrupt or disturb "the blanket of power over us." These efforts have led to alternative civic institutions like cultural centers that serve as networks for schools, women's groups, cooperatives, and NGOs. The destruction of tribal and clan-based leaderships has created a new cadre of leaders who have grown in confidence because they combine popular grassroots support with a genuine wish for an equitable coexistence with Israel. "Confident, educated, and above all open to the realities of Israel, these new men and women radiate a kind of hopeful security that exiles like myself envy" (*A*, p. 112). Is this form of partial, minoritarian affiliation, across class interests and gendered identities, the wave of the future for all of us—irrespective of nation, race, and culture—who hope to survive the destructive element?

Committing himself to the "undocumented turbulence" of the wretched of the earth of our times, Said echoes Frantz Fanon's descriptions of the "occult instability" of the decolonizing consciousness in the mid-twentieth-century wars of independence. Both Fanon and Said died of leukemia, almost half a century apart, in hospital beds on the East Coast of the United States, only a few hundred miles from each other. Both of them produced last books beckoning the world towards an aspirational "new" humanism. Fanon, however, wrote (or so he thought) with his foot on the threshold of a Third World of nations, on the verge of "start[ing] over a new history of man." Said could be persuaded of no such humanist haven. The "unsettled energy" of the times, or what he describes elsewhere as "the implacable energy of place and displacement," provides him with a double vision of history in which tragedy and transition, incarceration and emancipation seem to be part of the same unravelling thread of events. It is from the turbulence of wars, occupations, segregations, and evictions that there emerges a resistant hope that these unsettled energies of place and displacement will settle into a design for living with shared borders and contrapuntal histories. If oppression and destruction can tear down walls and destroy frontiers, then why can't those gates remain open, those spaces be deterritorialized in times of peace? It is as if hostility brings us closer to our neighbors in a deadly embrace than hospitality ever can. "Why do you think I'm so interested in the bi-national state?" Said asks the Israeli journalist Ari Shavit. "Because I want a rich fabric of some sort, which no one can fully comprehend, and no one can fully own. I never understood the idea of this is my place, and you are out. I do not appreciate going back to the origin, to the pure."[9]

A rich tapestry of visions and voices appears in a photograph that accompanies a prose poem in *After the Last Sky;* it is part of a series of descriptions of the interiors of Palestinian homes. The patterns of life and art that Said associates with the Palestinian experience—"broken narratives, fragmentary compositions, and self-consciously staged testimonials" (*A*, p. 38)—are recognizably modernist forms of narrative representation that ring true for the persecution of minorities. Said starts the sequence by turning to Freud's concept of the compulsion to repeat as a leitmotif of everyday life. In a loose translation of the demonic dance between repetition and the death drive, he suggests that the Palestinian's fundamental sense of loss and displacement repeats and refigures itself in rituals of excess: "too many

9. Said, "My Right of Return," interview with Ari Shavit, *Power, Politics, and Culture,* p. 457.

places at a table; too many pictures; too many objects; too much food. . . . We keep recreating the interior. . . . but it inadvertently highlights and preserves the rift or break fundamental to our lives" (*A*, p. 58). There is a slowness, a deferral, in this narrative of an interior life where the baroque elements of excess barely conceal the fear of repetition, the possibility that evacuation and exile may occur again. And yet, if the compulsion to repeat is the tragic sign of a fundamental rift or displacement, its *excessive* (and asymmetric) embellishments of unfurnished lives—too many carpets, pictures, figurines, flags, photographs—are more comedic in their collective, communitarian spirit of survival and celebration. "The rift is usually expressed as a comic dislocation," Said writes, which leaves us, once again, with a version of a question I posed earlier: What do all these parts add up to? parts of a home; parts of a past; parts of an interior life; parts of memory; parts of dispersed peoples? All part(s) of a larger pattern that repeatedly stages the problem of "those connections that allow us to see part and whole, that is the main thing: what to connect with, how, and how not?" (*HDC*, p. 78). What part do these partial connections play in providing us with some small, modest piece of knowledge that might help us to understand something about the shape of liberation?

An answer, I believe, is to be found in those interiors where the partial objects or symbols of a larger historic life continually vie for our attention, changing their locations and locutions, transiting from one narrative or phenomenal form to another. "Always infinitesimally varied, interiors will ultimately attract the attention of the outside observer—as it has caught Jean Mohr's eye" (*A*, p. 61). There is something fugal, a kind of polyphonic arrangement, in this repetition of peoples, things, images, and stories dedicated to the larger labor of memory and history. Sometimes this fugal figure is found in a rich tapestry or carpet of contrasting weaves; sometimes it hangs off the tongue or the page in a complex and constant transposition of the modalities of theme, character, and narrative person; sometimes it is heard in the polyphony of musical voices, in the contrapuntal arrangement of subjects and countersubjects. Each excessive element plays an equal part in the recall of memory and the remaking of a fragmented history: the carpet is of no greater value in this narrative than the photograph, or the broken doll, or the cherished teapot.

It is from Said's figurative descriptions of Palestinian interiors and interiority that we understand a certain measure of equality in representation that exists in the polyphonic voices and contrapuntal structures that make up the rich fabric of fugal music. Polyphony and contrapuntality are amongst Said's most commonly used poetic and political metaphors to describe the procedures of philological reception and resistance: "And so multiple identity, the polyphony of many voices playing off against each other, without, as I say, the need to reconcile them, just to hold them together, is what my work is all about."[10] Polyphonic music is, of course, a strict style with prescriptive formal procedures and progressions. But its enthralling impression of effortless improvisation—"something plastic and benign" (*ME*, p. 72)—comes from the way in which it structures and restructures an equitable, dialogic relationship between part and whole through the processes of repetition and counterpoint. I am tempted to suggest that even more than the sheer plurality and virtuosity of voices, polyphony provides us with a figurative vision of the possibilities of fairness and freedom in the midst of complex transitional structures. Is there a moral to be drawn from a musical form that might just illuminate the ethical and political norms by which we live? There is something resembling a democratic practice that runs through the fugal form and establishes the convention that several voices must, at different times, claim the character of a main part; that the contrapuntal process should express the feelings and aspirations of several peoples; and that the combination of subjects and structures ensures that each voice is answerable to the other.[11]

What, then, of the narrative of slowness? In developing this theme, I am aware that I may be making my own beginnings from what are, in the general scheme of things, only the odds and ends of Said's *oeuvre*. There is, however, a mention of slowness in Said's thoughts on musical elaboration, illustrated by a passage from Bruckner's Ninth Symphony, that is memorable in itself and would make a fitting memorial to the passing of Edward's life. As against the "administrative and executive authority" audible in the "finished perfection" of the sonata form, Said confesses to a preference for the contrapuntal elaborations of imitation, repetition, and ornamentation because there the process of transformation "can occur *slowly* not only because we affirm and reaffirm its repetition, its meandering course, but also because it too seems to be about the same process . . . something both reflective and circular" (*ME*, p. 102). And as I listened to that passage from Bruckner and reflected on the transformations that shaped Said's work a thought occurred to me: Supposing we considered death neither to be a cessation of life nor an afterlife, but a slowing down, a transformation that eases away from the administrative and executive burdens of life and labor and turns into the meandering ways of memory, the reflective surfaces of writing, the fluid embrace of music?

---

10. Said, "Criticism, Culture, and Performance," p. 99.

11. See *New Grove Dictionary of Music*, s.v. "polyphony." I have made a composite definition to suit my purposes here.

About Politics, Palestine, and Friendship: A Letter to Edward from Egypt

Lila Abu-Lughod

March 25, 2004

Dear Edward,

Sitting on the thatched terrace of a house made of mud brick, watching children chase birds out of the ripening wheat fields while their mothers harvest clover for sheep and water buffalo, listening to a distant clang announcing the seller of bottled gas, and enjoying the winter sunshine through the eucalyptus, I can hardly conjure the world you inhabited. Even though you spent your boyhood in Egypt, it was north, in a different part of this country. There, your school was so exclusive that being an Oriental in it carried a stigma. There, your apartment was furnished with antiques and dusted by servants. Here, children march off to school in crumpled beige uniforms and recite from dog-eared government textbooks.

When I ask people here if they have heard of you—people who know a lot about growing wheat, Indian irrigation pumps, medical problems, and the sorry state of the Egyptian economy—they struggle with the name. Edward Said? Nothing comes up, though they know every television actor who will appear in the serial being filmed now in the nearby pharaonic ruin and every political personage who pontificates on the news. And they know Palestine. Some know it directly, like the ninety-some-year-old I met the other day who was taken to Gaza to cook for the British during the Second World War. Most know it indirectly, like all the women who report to me each day how many people were killed by the Israelis in Palestine. They shake their heads, "God protect them. God give them strength."

Our friends here also know my father. Some remember his visit seven years ago. Others remember that when I was last here on a research trip, I was anxious about him. I traveled to Ramallah to see him when he came out of the hospital. I still see in various homes the posters of Al-Aqsa Mosque in Jerusalem that I brought as gifts, pinned up beside posters of Mecca, favorite Egyptian soccer teams, Arab pop stars, and cartoon bears. There is a gentle hesitation whenever I mention my father. A respect for the loss. It is this connection to my father and to Palestine that allows me to think about you here.

Your son brought some laughter to the numb group gathered at your funeral at Riverside Church in New York City when he told us how amazed he was that you managed to write so much when it seemed that you spent all your time talking on the telephone. My memories of life with my father also carry the familiar sounds of him talking on the phone—affectionate, angry, urgent, cajoling, mixing Arabic and English, talking politics. And you were the person my father talked to most.

I know your friendship began in Princeton, through music. I was just two when my father began graduate school there in the mid-1950s, still un-polished, with a thick accent and Arab nationalist sympathies. He had cho-sen Oriental studies at Princeton to work with Philip Hitti, the only modern Arab historian teaching in the United States. My father had come far in the barely six years since his expulsion from Jaffa, the city he was forced to flee when it fell to the Jewish forces, ten days before the destruction of Palestine and the declaration of the State of Israel. He had arrived in the United States by boat on borrowed money. His English was poor, though he had been among the smart students at Al-'Amiriyya High School (now called the Weitzman School). He savored the irony that he was a refugee with no future when he heard the news that he had passed his high school matriculation exams. The list was announced by Radio Israel; the Arab Department of Education no longer existed.

Like many an immigrant to the United States, my father had worked a variety of jobs in his first years, from mopping floors in a laundry to testing temperatures in a steel mill. He had also won a scholarship after his first year at a mediocre state university. In Chicago he had married my mother. She was beginning to develop in him an appreciation of, among other

Lᴉʟᴀ Aʙᴜ-Lᴜɢʜᴏᴅ is professor of anthropology and director of the Institute for Research on Women and Gender at Columbia University. She is the author of *Media Worlds: Anthropology on New Terrain* (2002), *Writing Women's Worlds: Bedouin Stories* (1993), and *Veiled Sentiments: Honor and Poetry in a Bedouin Society* (1986). Her most recent book is *Dramas of Nationhood: The Politics of Television in Egypt* (2005).

Ibrahim Abu-Lughod and Edward Said, 1986. Photos: Michelle Barrett.

things, classical music. The day you met, she had sent him to pick up free concert tickets made available to impoverished graduate students. You, a budding classical musician and a privileged Princeton undergraduate, were distributing the tickets. You moved in a different world from his, groomed by a New England prep school and, before that, Victoria College, where Egypt's wealthy, including Levantines, sent their sons and daughters. But when he asked you where you were from, and delicately confirmed that you were an Arab Palestinian, you began to talk.

You were to keep talking until May 23, 2001. This was the day my father died. But the reason the date is so fixed in my memory is that we had anxiously held it out to him, day after day, as the day you were to arrive. My father, suffering from what finally had been diagnosed, quite late, as lung cancer, was then living in Ramallah, the West Bank town to which he had moved in the early 1990s. His American passport entitled him, under Israeli authority, to stay for three-month stints as a tourist in his homeland. After forty years in the United States, he had "returned" to Palestine—not to his beloved Jaffa, too firmly within the borders of Israel, but to a part of Palestine that was just emerging (temporarily, as it has turned out) from direct Israeli military control. He was energized by the hope of contributing to a society beginning to breathe again. It had been a while since you'd last seen each other, but you talked on the telephone regularly. If the calls in early May focused more on medical reports than on the decisions of the Palestinian Authority or the latest Israeli outrage, you still talked about the world.

In the moments when my father was well enough to sit up, he planned busily for your visit. Everyone would want to see Edward, he said. He had to figure out how to arrange for you to see different circles of people without anyone feeling slighted and without burdening you. He knew you'd be tired from travel. My father extracted from me the reassurance that I knew how to make "Mom's Moroccan chicken." We abetted his excitement, though we knew his oxygen tank would alarm you and his weakness would hardly allow for the kind of dinner party he imagined—joking and holding forth, with the conversation lively, ranging back and forth from good-natured teasing to backbiting gossip to serious political argument. Out loud we counted the days until your arrival, hoping it would keep him going. Secretly we prayed that you would come sooner.

At the commemoration ceremony held for my father in Ramallah the day after his funeral in Jaffa, Mahmoud Darwish, the Palestinian poet, described my father's eagerness to see you as "the longing of a twin for his soul mate."[1] But you were in no way twins. What was this extraordinary

1. Mahmoud Darwish, "Ibrahim Abu-Lughod: The Path of Return Is the Path of Knowledge" (in Arabic), *Akhbar Yafa*, 31 May 2001, p. 4.

friendship? What did you give each other? What did you see in each other? To understand this friendship is to see a side of you that perhaps was not visible to colleagues in America who knew you only as a brilliant and intimidating literary critic, or to those around the world who saw you as being an outspoken public intellectual who kept the truth of Palestine alive.

It is hard for anyone to know, really, what goes on between friends. What I saw was mutual respect. And loyalty. I saw the trusting camaraderie born of a shared passion to use the mind to grasp the political predicament in which you, as Arabs and Palestinians, found yourselves. You both spoke out with consistency and integrity, though my father was sometimes more accommodating because of his involvement in realpolitik. I saw in both of you an incredible confidence, perhaps born of desperation, that your actions could affect the world. You wanted to change history by writing, though later in life you would try to make a difference by bringing Palestinian and Israeli musicians together; my father was always more effective through the people he talked to, one by one, and through his ability to mobilize them through the institutions he brought into being.

My father respected talent and had a gift for putting Arabs and Palestinians to work for the cause. You were in another league, really, although when my father began to draw you into the Association of Arab-American University Graduates (an association he had helped found after the 1967 war), you were still an awkward public speaker. You would never have my father's fiery oratory, his easy warmth, or his humor. But you had formidable intellectual power, and you worked like a madman. My father would proudly take credit for bringing you into Palestinian politics, especially the struggle in the United States against anti-Arab sentiment, misinformation, and hostile policy. The key moment was when he asked you to contribute an essay to a special issue of a journal after the 1967 war. You wrote for my father what he always recalled as an incredible essay—about the image of the Arab in the West. This was the germ of what became your most transformative book, *Orientalism*.

In your memoir, you told us that your father steered clear of politics and your refined mother pushed you to opera.[2] Your own brilliance and nervous energy gave you a stellar academic career. But my father helped secure a place for you, a sometimes prickly thoroughbred, in the Arab political community. He drew you deep into conversation with politically committed Palestinians living in Beirut, Syria, Tunis, Qatar, Jordan, and London. You thanked him, in your eulogy in Ramallah, for introducing you to so many

2. See Edward W. Said, *Out of Place: A Memoir* (New York, 1999).

interlocutors and dear friends. Was it through my father that you got involved in the Palestinian National Council and developed your ambivalent relationship to Yasir Arafat, the leader you would later condemn unsparingly for his use of the Oslo accords to cling to personal power, bending to Israel's will and forfeiting the rights of his people?

Arafat had been important to my father. Someone had introduced them in Cairo in August 1970, just as the Palestine Liberation Organization (PLO) was emerging. My father remembers looking straight at him and asking: "Mr. Arafat, what role do you see for people like me who are living outside? We are intellectuals, working with ideas at institutions. What role do you see for us in the revolution?" Arafat's answer, in that heady language of the era, stuck with my father. "Doctor, when we began our revolution, we were Palestinians sitting in Kuwait or Qatar thinking, 'What can we do for Palestine?' We decided to make a revolution . . . . We organized ourselves and here we are." He continued, "Now, for you and your friends, think about what you can do. If you need help from us to do what you want to do, let us know. But it is for you to decide how you can contribute to this revolution, which is yours. How do you contribute to the liberation of Palestine?"[3]

Arafat invited him to attend the upcoming meeting of the Palestinian National Council. From then on, my father felt himself more a Palestinian. He taught political science, he had wide interests in nationalism and liberation movements, he continued to listen to Vivaldi, and he tried to keep wayward children on track. But he spoke widely, wrote, and also flew to New York to sit in the PLO suite at the United Nations' sessions where men drafted resolutions and strategized about how to get the world to recognize the Palestinian plight. Bottles of Johnnie Walker Black on the table, lots of smoke, and intense masculine argument. Were you there? I don't remember. But you were there as a fellow member of the Palestinian National Council in meetings in Amman, Cairo, and Algiers. When they drafted the declaration of statehood in Algiers in 1988, I expect you backed my father, the father of three daughters and one son, when he supported women's equal right to pass on Palestinian nationality to their children.

Sitting next to my father, you were a featured speaker, year after year, at the annual meetings of the Association of Arab-American University Graduates where academic papers were presented and politics analyzed. The two of you helped found the *Arab Studies Quarterly,* an academic journal intended as an alternative to Zionist and Orientalist scholarship on the

---

3. Quoted in Hisham Ahmed-Fararjeh, *Ibrahim Abu-Lughod: Resistance, Exile, and Return* (Birzeit, 2003), p. 115.

Arab world. And you wrote and wrote, encouraged and applauded by my father: books like *The Question of Palestine* and *Covering Islam;* prescient essays like "Permission to Narrate," written on the occasion of the Israeli invasion of Lebanon in 1982. You showed in that article how talk of terrorism conveniently—deliberately—blocked any narration of the histories that could lay bare the roots and reason of violence.

I was touched when your elegy to my father in the *London Review of Books* was titled "My Guru."[4] You were the star. You were the giant. My father was very smart, and he certainly understood politics; he was also a charismatic teacher and an energetic participant in what he called "village politics"—university life. But his devotion to the Arab community in the United States led him to accumulate Man of the Year plaques from dozens of Arab American and Palestinian organizations, not honorary degrees from prestigious universities. His energies went into trying to make things happen, especially in the Arab world, whether the Palestinian Open University that UNESCO had asked him to plan (and that an Israeli cluster bomb on his Beirut balcony, and all that came with the invasion in 1982, prevented him from establishing) or, much later, the edited volume of proceedings from the "Landscapes of Palestine" conference that he organized at Birzeit University, in Palestine. You gave the keynote address at that conference and brought your inspiring friend W. J. T. Mitchell, editor of *Critical Inquiry,* something my father was still excited about years later. I was humbled to find you describing my father as "an authority for all important things I did as an intellectual."[5]

If you cherished my father's friendship, my father was fiercely loyal to you. He appreciated your work and delighted in your achievements. I saw an interviewer on the Al-Jazeera television program *Guest and Issue* in 2000 ask my father's opinion of a statement made by one Palestinian professor that there are two models for dealing with the Palestinian political situation. The first model was said to be Dr. Ibrahim Abu-Lughod, who had decided to return and to wage a new form of daily struggle on the land of Palestine. Then there was the other model, Dr. Edward Said, abroad, whose "extremist" response was to talk only about his disgust with the current Palestinian political line. "Do you think," the interviewer asked, "that there really are two models for dealing with the political situation?"

My father said flatly, "I don't think that at all." He refused the invidious comparison. He defended you fairly, recognizing and respecting your differences. He explained that his Arab roots and Arab commitment had re-

4. See Said, "My Guru," *London Review of Books,* 13 Dec. 2001, pp. 19–20.
5. Said, "If I Had Had a Brother, He Would Not Have Been More True, Gentle, and Loving Than Ibrahim" (in Arabic), *Akhbar Yafa,* 31 May 2001, p. 4.

mained constant through the work he did. He noted that though his career (as a professor of political science at various universities) was in the United States, he had also worked in Egypt and Beirut. You, he noted, had been educated in America, where your academic work kept you. Turning things around, my father used the occasion to hold you up as a model for Palestinians. He pointed out that you did come to Palestine, though your work was elsewhere. And to work elsewhere, he added, "is the right of every Palestinian, no matter where. That is the transnational character of the Palestinian people." My father then praised you as "a distinguished model for what the diaspora can do for Palestine." First, "what it can do in the confrontation with Israel" but also in its criticism of the Palestinian Authority. "As a Palestinian, he also has the right, the complete right," he said of you, "to express his opinion about what's going on politically in the lands of the Palestinian Authority. That is the sacred right of every Palestinian. He exercises it. But he exercises it outside because he exercises all his rights outside. His is the worldly model . . . . But he is part of this country, just as I was part of it before I came back." He ended, "But, anyway, we are not two models. There are many models for the Palestinian people."

You and my father were comrades in a search for justice for Palestinians. You were also friends. I don't think you talked to each other about family matters much, but you appreciated each others' insights, talents, and humanity. I saw on several occasions your great capacity for love, you who could not suffer fools, were pitiless toward those who crossed you, and could be impatient with your own family. In your extraordinary elegy you spoke in the same breath about my father and your other friend Eqbal Ahmad. What a troika. He passed away two years before my father, in Pakistan. This was the country to which he had, like my father, "returned" after a life spent in the United States. It hadn't escaped any of you that his location in Pakistan as a refugee from India was the result of one of those colonial partitions so popular in the late 1940s (India and Pakistan, apartheid in South Africa, Israel and Palestine) that was not so different from the one you and my father suffered. For me, growing up, Eqbal was adored, the only other friend of my father's besides you who could keep us riveted at the dining room table when the talk turned to politics.

At the memorial service for Eqbal at the Asia Society in New York, my father spoke gratefully of what Eqbal had done for the Palestinians through his acute political analyses and his warnings about the dangers of provincial nationalism. You ended on a more human note, saying, "So much has been said about Eqbal's qualities: his generosity, his brilliance, his honesty, his commitment to justice and truth, his great human and pedagogic powers

... Eqbal the activist and speaker .... I want to conclude this extraordinary occasion, if I might, by recalling one experience which moved me and my family greatly." You told us about how he had come every day for two months to sit with you after you returned from the hospital, sick and weak from a difficult experimental treatment. "Most of the time," you said, "I was not able to speak or even to stay awake. I was in pain, and I was suffering. But there, across the room, was Eqbal, sometimes nursing a drink, sometimes not. Sitting there quietly, available to me, to Mariam, and my children." He was a friend to you, and a guru as well. You described how you used to call him Mawlana (religious teacher) and he used to call you Sayf al-Islam (Sword of Islam)—"the most inappropriate titles that ever went between friends." Then you added, "But it was, I think, a sign of our very deep friendship and the love that we had for each other."

My father was to be the next friend you lost. May 23, 2001. You missed seeing him by hours. So instead of being feted at dinner parties, you had to walk with us, with hundreds of people from all over Palestine, through the streets of Jaffa to bring my father to the cemetery overlooking the sea that he had loved to swim in as a boy. We left him there. And you pressed on. You were not silent when, months later, Israeli tanks rolled into Ramallah, a savage bombardment devastated Jenin, assassinations alternated with invasions, and the lies continued. Yet you wrote that you felt diminished by the loss of my father.

I, like so many others, now feel diminished by the silencing of your voice. You three were remarkable men forged in the colonial crucible and fired unevenly by the enthusiasms of liberation movements. Driven by your burdens, you gave yourselves to the world. I like to imagine the three of you now sitting up there in heaven, drinking Johnnie Walker Black and talking politics. I sit here on the earthen terrace with the sunset warming the pharaonic temple across the field, wondering how to carry on your work. The first step, I know, is to keep talking about Palestine.

Love,

Lila

Interpreting a Distinction

Akeel Bilgrami

In a distinction derived from Vico—but developed along very distinctive lines of his own—between the concept of origins and the concept of beginnings, Edward Said raises a whole range of fundamental issues: about the nature of writing and indeed more generally about the nature of human freedom.[1]

Vico had spoken of how the very notion of a chosen people, by the privilege it bestowed on them, protected them from the acts of imagination and intellect by which they might probe their own origins. These acts, which since his time came to be described in terms of genealogy but which Vico himself described as divination, were acts that acknowledged a fundamental fact about those who are allowed their indulgence—that they were always in history, stuck in it, outside of the privilege of the sacred domain, and therefore these probings were essentially the Gentile acts of an enforced secularity. The discipline of history (and indeed of philosophical anthropology and the very idea of what later came to be called *Geisteswissenschaften*) therefore was by its nature a secular one.

Said's use of this distinction is suggestive and varied. In this brief paper, I will only be able to explore one strand of suggestion, ignoring many other

The ideas presented in this brief paper were first presented in the three graduate seminars that Edward Said and I gave on the broad subject of historicism and interpretation at Columbia University. I am grateful to him for his responses there and also to Carol Rovane and James Miller for their comments on a draft of this paper.

1. See Edward W. Said, *Beginnings: Intention and Method* (1975; New York, 1997); hereafter abbreviated *B*. The distinction is made throughout the work, but it is most explicit in the preface and chapter 1. For Vico, see his *The New Science*, trans. T. G. Bergin and M. H. Fisch (Ithaca, N.Y., 1988). The distinction is made in many parts of the book; see p. 103, just to give one good instance of it.

more familiar and well-mined Saidian themes, such as the contrasts he draws between filiation and affiliation, repetition and departure, social constraint and individual talent, and ignoring too his vast range of references from Marx and before to Auerbach and after.

The contrast I want to focus on is the one he himself strikingly expresses by saying: "As consistently as possible I use *beginning* as having the more active meaning, and *origin* the more passive one: 'X *is the origin of* Y' while 'The beginning A *leads to* B'" (*B*, p. 6). The essential passivity that he finds in the notion of origin is his way of developing Vico's understanding of the chosen people. Said says that this latter status necessarily amounts to a passive condition, the condition of *being* chosen. And now Vico's point about divination (acts of inquiry into origins) being forbidden to one by the certitude of that status of being placed outside of history and contingency can also be redescribed in terms of passivity. It is a deprivation of agency because the *acts* of beginning are excluded by the passivity inherent in the very notion of origin. The notion of divination in Vico is therefore broadened by this to include all acts of beginning; as a result his claim about how we must understand the secular probings that will constitute the discipline of history and of philosophical anthropology becomes, in Said, a point more broadly about writing and the exercise of imagination or inquiry itself.

But notice a curious thing. The contrast he has himself made between passive and active offers Said a parallel contrasting term to *being* chosen, which is *choosing*. But he refuses the offer. He is very careful in the quoted passage not to make his contrast quite so schematically. The idiom he adopts instead is one of *leads to*—something at once more unobvious and less voluntaristic. That is a point of some significance. Let me explore it.

The choice of "leads to," instead of something more unambiguously voluntaristic in describing the active voice of beginning, is significant in Said's own mind presumably because—as he seems to announce in the subtitle of the book—beginnings are constrained by the *intention* of the agent who writes and imagines; and intentions bring with them a *method*, a method of inquiry. Now, it is true that Said himself explicitly introduces the notion of intention in tandem with beginnings in order to escape the passivity of origins; that is, it is his way of introducing the full and final possibilities of *agency* that are denied when one speaks of origins and of the chosen people

A K E E L B I L G R A M I is Johnsonian Professor of philosophy and director of the Heyman Center for the Humanities at Columbia University. He is the author of *Belief and Meaning* (1992) and two forthcoming books: *Self-Knowledge and Resentment* and *Politics and the Moral Psychology of Identity*.

living only in a privileged, sacred history. The idea here, one assumes, is that intentions are on the active rather than the passive side of things because they are states of mind that don't befall one; rather, one *forms* intentions. But what I am stressing just as much as the agency is that intention for him brings with it a notion of "leads to" and in particular leads to in line with a method, and that *constrains* the way in which one might understand the notion of agency itself—as something less than pure choice and invention. It is this philosophical pulling in of the reins on agency even as he insists on it (already displayed in how the subtitle of the book immediately qualifies its title) that underlies and allows his appeal to agency to be unembarrassed by the fact of other sorts of constraining phenomena, phenomena such as filiation, repetition, and so on, which he then exploits with shrewd and rich critical resourcefulness throughout his career. But it is worth focusing just on the underlying philosophy that allows all this.

At various points, Said conceptually joins origins with *originality* and *still* pursues its distinctness from beginnings. Why? Is not originality a more natural property of one's acts rather than of what is given to one? Why, then, does originality fall on the side of origin, which is passive, rather than on the side of beginnings? It cannot just be because of the *surface* grammar of the cognates (origins, so therefore originality). That would be—well—shallow. There must be a point of greater depth at stake. Said does not take this question up, but, if we make the appropriate interpretative and dialectical links within his own framework, we can construct on his behalf a point of some real conceptual penetration.

When he refuses to pay the compliment of originality to writing and imagination conceived as acts of beginning, he does so saying that they deserve the more modest description: points of departure. The assigning of agency to beginnings *via intention* (rather than invention) now impresses with its relevance. It is this assignment that makes it quite incoherent to place originality on the side of beginnings. For it is built into the very idea of originality that one cannot *intend* to be original. That literally makes no sense. Just to make the point with an illustration, it is precisely this nonsense, for instance, that accounts for the discomfort we feel in reading the famously flamboyant beginning of Rousseau's *Confessions*.[2] It might seem at first sight that we are just a little embarrassed by its egotism, but in fact we are unsettled not by the boast of his announcing his originality so much as by the conceptual oddity of his announcing his originality as a *goal*, as what he is setting out to do or be.

What Aristotle said of pleasure—that it is an experience or property provided *in* or *by* other things we pursue, but it cannot by itself be an object

---

2. See Jean-Jacques Rousseau, *The Confessions*, trans. J. M. Cohen (London, 1953).

of pursuit—is more acutely true of originality. All an act of beginning, in Said's sense, can set out to do, all it can do by way of announced *intention*, is to say what by one's own lights is worth saying—because it is, by one's own lights, roughly and approximately true, true of one's experience, true of how one perceives the world and others, and so on. So if, contra Rousseau, one can have no other goal or intention in beginning an inquiry but to say what is (by one's lights, of course; what other lights are there?) true, then it is these lights that also then implicitly provide the *method* of one's inquiry. Originality may of course *be* a property of what one says. That is not being denied. All that is being denied is that what one says can be *intended* as original. What one says *is* original, if no one has said it before or said it in just that way or said it with the same right and conviction and persuasion. But these are all circumstances independent of what is intended by one. They are circumstances relating to how what one says relates to what others have said.[3] Not being something one can intend, originality can only be a fallout of these other things that may (or may not) hold of what one can and does intend to say. In that sense, appearances to the contrary, it falls on the passive rather than the active side. It is Said's stress on intention as a constitutive feature of beginnings therefore that accounts for why that is so.

But there is danger here. In giving such emphasis to intention and method, one might lose what there is to the *freedom* of writing and thought. Said himself says repeatedly that intention and method bring with them a path of inquiry; they "lead to" places that are generated by the intention and the method. Wherein lies the agency, then? Is it not all given over to a causality, even if it is not one of a sacred origin? Have we not lost our freedom, only this time to our own human natures and secular social and discursive contexts within which intentions and methods are generated and determined? This problem, which surfaces in this early book, recurs for Said in all of his work, and indeed James Clifford in a now well-known review of *Orientalism* chastises him for the pervasive inconsistency of having all sorts of humanistic aspirations that demand agency, while at the same time surrendering precisely agency in his thrall to a Foucauldian historicist framework in that work.[4] In his way, Said responded to this dilemma

3. I suppose if one knew what *everyone* else had said, one could without incoherence intend to say something different and original, but even such an intention (based on the scarcely human condition of omniscience) could not be a *self-standing* one. One would also have to intend to say what was worth saying for other reasons—that it got things right by one's lights, for instance—else the intention to be original would be, if not incoherent, some form of idle vanity, a caricature of romanticist aspiration.

4. See James Clifford, "On *Orientalism*," *The Predicament of Culture: Twentieth-Century Ethnography, Literature, and Art* (Cambridge, Mass., 1988), and Said, *Orientalism* (New York, 1978).

through all his work, and before he died he returned to address it (among other things) in his book on humanism. But, already in *Beginnings*, there is an explicit awareness of the difficulty and the need to respond to it, even if the actual response is somewhat obscure and less than fully developed. Properly elaborated, however, it says enough if not to preempt Clifford's anxiety then to set him on the path to doing so.

Two kinds of beginnings or aspects of beginning are distinguished by Said, and they are named transitive and intransitive.

He says of the first: "One leads to the project being realized: this is the transitive aspect of the beginning—that is, beginning with (or for) an anticipated end" (*B*, p. 72). A little later he adds, "One, which I call temporal and transitive, foresees a continuity that *flows from it*. This kind of beginning . . . allows us to initiate, to direct, to measure time to construct work, to discover, to produce knowledge" (*B*, p. 76; my emphasis). All this is just recapitulating the "leads to" idiom of following through on an intention in inquiry according to a method. If this is all there is to beginning, the danger of loss of freedom would be realized.

The other kind or aspect of beginning is motivated explicitly as a resistance to just this outcome. He says: "The other aspect [of beginning] retains for the beginning its identity as *radical* starting point: the intransitive and conceptual aspect, that which has no object but its own constant clarification" (*B*, pp. 72–73). And then adds a little later,

> In attempting to push oneself further and further back to what is only a beginning, a point that is stripped of every use but its categorization in the mind as beginning, one is caught in a tautological circuit of beginnings about to begin. This is the other kind of beginning, the one I called intransitive and conceptual. It is very much a creature of the mind, very much a bristling paradox, yet also very much a figure of thought that draws special attention to itself. Its existence cannot be doubted, yet its pertinence is wholly to itself. [*B*, p. 77]

This passage and others like it are not as transparent as one would have liked. What is clear is that Said feels the need to introduce the second aspect of beginning in order to resist the dangers of his own way of elaborating the first aspect. But it is not obvious how the infinite regress of beginning that is being proposed can by itself resist the threat of the loss of freedom. Why, it might be asked, does it not in fact deepen the difficulty? The trouble with an infinite regress is that it can cut both ways. It may seem to resist the inevitable, "leading to" ends as determined by the method generated by intention because it leaves us always at the beginning in an endless regress, but what freedom it would register in doing so is one that goes nowhere. It is freedom as stultification. That does not seem to be what one wants from the notion of agency in the first place. And, in any case, Said's own insistence that the rhetoric surrounding beginnings be deflated to points of departure implies that a regress should not be given the weight that his second, intransitive aspect of beginning places on it.

Other remarks, however, suggest a more fruitful line of resistance (and they in fact even suggest a more sympathetic reading of the passages already cited, though I will not be able to say how they suggest this in this brief discussion). One in particular comes close to saying what is crucially needed: "*From the point of view of the writer,* however, his writing—as he does it—is perpetually at the beginning" (*B*, p. 74; my emphasis). If we focus on the second half of this remark, we make no advance on the issue. That some writing or inquiry should perpetually be at the beginning, I have said, is either an obscure idea or (to the extent that it is clear) an idea implying a regressive aspect that does no particular favors to Said's own attempt at resisting the difficulties raised by the first intentional and methodical (what he calls the transitive) aspect of beginnings. But the first half of the remark makes a vital difference to how we might understand and reorient this otherwise disappointing second half. "From the point of view of the writer" is the real source of the resistance that is needed.

What is really important about Said's insight about there having to be two aspects of beginnings is not that the first leads forward and the second is regressive but rather that there are two perspectives or *points of view* upon one's acts of beginning. They are viewable from the outside, from the perspective of reflection, from the third-person point of view, but they are also viewable from the point of view of the agent (in his quoted remark, the particular agent is of course the writer), that is to say, the *first-person* point of view. When viewed from the third-person point of view the "leads to" idiom provides a natural description of it. That is what threatens with the loss of freedom. But from the first-person point of view, "leads to" is a quite inapt description.

What needs amending or reorienting is the claim that when one brings onto center stage the first-person point of view (in Said's words, "from the point of view of the writer"), one is generating a regress or an inescapable vortex of beginnings. A proper appreciation of the centrality of the first-person point of view in fact allows us to escape the vortex and arrest the regress. Such a proper appreciation is sometimes hard to come to because we can lose sight of the fact that one can take a *third*-person point of view *on oneself*, and when one does so one is not oneself in the agential or first-personal mode; one is not a subject but rather the object of one's own gaze. The regress is something that one only falls into if one keeps looking at one's beginnings from the *third*-person point of view (reflecting on oneself from the outside) and realizing that each last reflection requires another. Such a regress is precisely finessed if one *switches points of view*, switches from self-perception or reflection on oneself and one's beginnings to the perspective of *being an agent,* the point of view from which one *makes* (or acts) the beginning rather than reflects on it.

I have said that Said spoils his own insight captured in his phrase "from the point of view of the writer" by how he completes the remark in which that phrase occurs. This happens again and again in all the passages where he elaborates on the intransitive aspect of beginning. How should we diagnose this tendency on his part? I think it has to do with the fact that in this work he has an imperfect grip on the role of intention and method that he so insightfully introduces into the very idea of a beginning. The fault line of reasoning in the tendency runs roughly as follows: The notions of intention and method are to be described in the "leads to" idiom of the transitive mode of beginning. But, in doing so, we are in danger of losing the freedom of writing and thought. To resist this danger, we must find some notion or aspect of beginning that excludes intention and method for which that offending idiom is apt, and we can do that only if we acknowledge an inescapable regress of beginnings, the intransitive mode of beginning.

The conclusion of this (fault) line of reasoning is quite uncompulsory, if it should turn out that from the *first*-person point of view intention and method are *not* aptly described in the "leads to" idiom. So, it is not—as he argues—that we need to supplement the intentional notion or aspect of beginning by another notion or aspect of beginning that abandons intention because intention always implies an agency-threatening "leads to" idiom. Rather what we need is to find a way of denying that intention always implies a "leads to" idiom. And the first half of his remark about the writer's or first-person point of view offers him just such a way. From the first-person point of view, an intention does not *lead to* any action that "flows from" (to use Said's own words above) the intention with the guidance of the method (the transitive aspect). That causal idiom of "leads to," "flows from," and so on is quite apt while the point of view on the intention is one of the self-*observer* rather than the actor, and so on, while it is the point of view of the subject *as object* rather than as agent. But the idiom is mismatched with the first-person point of view because in the first person one asks not what action *will my intention lead to* but what action *should* or *ought* I to do to be in *accord* with my intention and its implied method. Thus the switch from the third- to the first-person point of view that Said rightly demands in that remark will only generate a regress if one (not having seen the full point of the switch) is still tethered to the idiom of causality, of "leading to." But it will generate no such thing if, in full appreciation of the switch, one switches also to notions of ought or should and accord, which are the *normative* rather than the *causal* idiom that agency demands.

When I began the consideration of this issue, I applauded Said for having refused the empty and unexplained voluntaristic term *choosing* to express the contrast that *beginnings* provides with the being chosen of origins. The talk of intention and method instead of choosing was his way of making that refusal. But in elaborating the notions of intention and method only from a third-person point of view, he allows those notions to be exhaustively understood in the "leads to" idiom of causality. And even when he insightfully brings the first-person point of view into focus, as in the remark I cited, he does not see through to how this insight necessarily brings with it the deep relevance of value or norm to agency.

This relevance, as I said, consists in the fact that when we view intentions from the first-person point of view of the agent we cannot see our intentions in the "leads to" causal mode. That is to say, we cannot step outside of the first-person point of view *while we are in it* and view ourselves from the outside, from a third-person point of view. In a word, we cannot both be *agents* and at the same time be *observers* or predictors of ourselves and what our minds will cause us or "lead" us to do. While we are agents we ask what *ought* we to do, and we say what we are *committed* to doing by our intentions. Talk of oughts and commitments, however, is paradigmatically a normative and evaluative way of talking.

By normative and evaluative talk, I don't necessarily by any means have in mind moralistic talk. It is a confusion (at any rate, reductive) to think that the realm of value is exhausted by the realm of the moral. The commitments in question here are generated by one's own intentions, not by something external to us as morality is often taken to be. But it is normative all the same. Consider the most trivial of examples of an intention. I intend to take my umbrella when I go out. But, let's say, when the time comes I don't take my umbrella. In that case, by the lights of my intention, I did something *wrong*. I failed to live up to the commitment generated by the intention. This is not a moral wrong. But that we can all the same use the term *wrong* quite appropriately makes it uncontroversially an evaluative phenomenon. The triviality of the example may show that evaluative and normative vocabulary does not always have to have a high profile. Weightier examples may increase the stature of the profile, but even the trivial examples reveal that there is an *intrinsic* link between intention and value.

And the point of contrast with all this is that while we are observers of ourselves and not agents, while we have a third- rather than a first-person angle on ourselves, we ask or say what we will be *led to* do by our intentions rather than what we should or ought to do, given our intentions. That is a nonnormative, causal way of talking. And the two ways of talking (normative and causal) are strictly incommensurate. We *cannot straddle* both ways of talking. We can only switch from one to the other. The impossibility that the cannot here is conveying is analogous to the impossibility in our perception of that notorious figure in Wittgenstein: we can see it as a duck and we can see it as a rabbit but we cannot see it as a duck *while* we see it as a rabbit. To see the one rather than the other, one has to make a switch in perspective or point of view. Wittgenstein in that example of course was not meaning to point to perspectives of the first person and the third person, agent and observer. So I invoke him only by way of analogy. But the analogy is a good one because it conveys that a perspectival shift is required in each case.

It is because Said does not see through to this last step, implied by his own insight in invoking "the point of view of the writer" in that cited remark, that he lands us in the end with the impoverished options of the empty rhetoric of choosing versus the agency-threatening causal idiom of "leads to." But if the interpretations and diagnoses offered in this brief discussion are right, we are in a position now to say that what is needed to explain and fill out the otherwise idle voluntaristic idiom of choosing is to conceptually link it along these lines with norm and value. Now it is no longer a dogmatically asserted voluntarism; it is *one with* our normative, deliberative exercises involved in inquiry or writing or action.

I say "*one* with" and mean it. We have, anciently, thought there are two mysteries: the very possibility of free agency in a causal universe and the very place of value in a naturalistic world. If I am right, these are the *same* mystery. And reducing two mysteries to one is surely some sort of progress.

This normative and evaluative dimension *built into* the very idea of agency and intention is what is struggling to get out in Said's insight that something about the first-person point of view will provide the resistance to his transitive and causal aspects of beginnings that threaten freedom and agency. Because it doesn't quite get out, there is all that unhelpful talk of an infinite and perpetual regress of beginnings. That talk distracts from the fact that questions asked and assertions made about one's intentions from the first-person point of view (unlike from the third-person point of view) are not predictive; they are evaluative and speak to one's commitments rather than one's causal tendencies. It is really only where agency and value (intention and ought) join that Clifford's anxiety about the tensions in Said's twin commitments to historicism (causality, "leads to," and so on) and humanism will be calmed.[5] There is much more to be said here of course, and I regret that I must end, having hardly begun.

5. Those who have all along assumed that what made the human or social sciences special was that they were not value-free were making a quite correct assumption. But because they did not always dig deep enough, they were always vulnerable to the objection over the years that the natural sciences were also value-laden, in some broad sense. My paper can be seen as a brief effort (on behalf of Said) at saying something about the foundations of that correct assumption, something that because it stresses the link between value and the first-person point of view of agency is *not* vulnerable in the same way.

Continuing the Conversation

Paul Bové

Edward Said's presence made complacency impossible. From the first time I heard him lecture on Islamic theories of history and rhetoric to our last conversation about a trend in British historiography that admires imperialists' suffering more than is good for us, through those meetings, emails, phone calls, interviews, and occasional exchanges of offprints, Edward made it impossible to be satisfied. We should not misunderstand: he took and gave great pleasure. His learning, wit, even his angry rhetoric and relentless analysis exist within the world of intellectual pleasure, of commitment to forming oneself and one's society as occasions to live well. Moreover, he made people around him—me, at least—come to love criticism as his great teacher Blackmur had taught us: criticism is an act of love, and like writing it is the response to what has come before, to what is coming into being even now.

Never did Said, for all his worry about the Middle East and his study of European empire and Orientalism, stop thinking about the U.S. More than once, as all know, he lashed out at the PLO and the PA for their failure to study and understand the U.S. Furthermore, he understood that given the imbalance of power the directions of U.S. culture and policy would support or damage not only the political fate of states but also the life possibilities of entire civilizations. For an exile, criticism involves love for all the world, but it requires the clearest description, analysis, and judgment of power's realities, especially its unjust imbalances. The critic loves freedom enough and depends so much upon its possibility as a condition for its own exis-

I want to thank my *Boundary 2* colleagues—Joseph Buttigieg, Ronald Judy, Aamir Mufti, and Lindsay Waters—for commenting on this paper.

tence that he must speak truthfully, even harshly, to protect it. Edward knew that much depends upon the American democratic experiment because the nature of power makes its fate matter for all around the world. Said's worry about the world impact of the U.S. brought him to write *Humanism and Democratic Criticism.* In it, he continues a conversation begun long ago when, as his memoir makes clear, he came to that strange land of his father's citizenship and began the task of reading it, rewriting it, and helping the rest of us struggle to maintain its best elements. Because criticism is the fearless, continuous play of intellectual pleasure and love—Socrates is always in Said—then *Humanism and Democratic Criticism,* so critical of certain aspects of the U.S., is a book of great inventive justice. With it, he guides those who would assure that the U.S. does all it can to enrich and enhance the complexity of human life and culture by seeing, understanding, and battling possession by its own worst demons.

Humanism and Democratic Criticism is a lesson for America. It has epistolary force. It warns that America, which is the last remaining superpower, is nothing less than a threat to thought itself; but it embraces another America, which is radical in its desire for freedom and blessed by its intersecting cultures and histories. The battle for America, which is nothing less than what this book is about, is also a battle for much of the world, and, without any hyperbole, I say it is a book about the survival of the human species as a form of mind interested in and capable of knowing itself and its works and of desiring freedom and liberty.

As I read this book, so many things struck me that for quite a while it disabled me. It is a book that lets a reader start anywhere and follow it to almost any place in current life and politics as well as anywhere in history and knowledge. Above all, however, I found and continue to find it to be the most compelling reading of the consequences of not successfully counterpoising the neoconservative revolution that has seized control of U.S. state and a great deal of American cultural power—in addition to the partial control of economy and technology—and through these things, much of the world.

On a very few occasions, Edward Said mentions the neoconservatives and, for several paragraphs, rightly ridicules the late Allan Bloom and his sponsors, including Saul Bellow. But the critique of what underlies the neoconservatives and the U.S. policy of preemptive war and domestic right-wing political

PAUL BOVÉ is professor of English at the University of Pittsburgh and editor of *Boundary 2.* He is the author of, most recently, *Early Postmodernism: Foundational Essays* (1995) and the editor of *Edward Said and the Work of the Critic: Speaking Truth to Power* (2000).

maximalism is very textured and ubiquitous, deeply meaningful and relent-less in mapping extreme dangers and suggesting needed alternatives. Said quotes Spitzer to the effect that rereadings will produce a sense of a work's sun, its authorial center, its "etymology," with the vision of the author taken as itself the "etymon." Said always admirably insists that readers must re-sponsibly assert their interpretation and judgment knowing all along that the fallen, historical, and if you will tragic limitation of human perspective never produces a final reading. Yet each strong reading presents itself as authori-tative, and what I would like to assert here—since there is no time for analytic demonstration—is simply that this book best maps the ubiquitous forces and capillary realities that form the present moment's cultural and political dom-inant as a threat to historicist human being.

And it does this because Edward Said formed himself as a person whose closeness to language allowed him to embed and expose a range of inter-locking realities that critics otherwise rarely represent. I do not mean that others do not address the problems of religious fundamentalism or Hay-ekian neoliberalism. What I mean rather is that Said's book dramatizes the way a certain mind works, how it reads, how it is formed in relation to language and awareness, how it reconstructs the relations of culture and politics with an attention to the notated nuances that in our time so define the complexity of culture, knowledge, and politics. Said invokes the figure in the carpet to weave an incomplete but magisterial pattern. His vision generously aspires to inclusion and critique based on knowledge and rests on preternatural skills of composition and a sensibility resulting from a life-long exercise of his faculties upon and in language—the privileged common material practice of historical human life.

Said wrote *Humanism and Democratic Criticism* at a time when neocon-servative aspirants seized power on a well-prepared cultural, intellectual, and political terrain—a favorite figure of this book because, for Said, politics has to do principally with occupying and leaving territory. If we had any doubt that the current political regime intends to occupy territories once and for all and aspires to put an end to the historical transformations de-fining an immigrant culture and a migrant world order, then this book dis-pels them. Philological criticism begins with a text and reader but never rests until as much as possible of the expanding and interlocking contexts and conditions for writing and reading stand exposed for pleasure, edu-cation, and judgment. In this book, the exilic authorial voice achieves that love for all the world promised in leaving behind one country or one iden-tity. Let me be clear: Said's voice does not achieve a sort of universal vision of the world as it is; on the contrary, it stands against such a possibility in large part because it sees that the effort to impose such a vision through dehumanizing power threatens freedom and the species itself.

This last point requires amplification. Never could we accuse Said of pessimism, of the belief that resistance and human historical agency might be, once and for all, arrested by the applications of dominant power. He testifies for us that his experience of resistant people, in Palestine and elsewhere, assures heroic resistance in the struggle for freedom and control. Nonetheless, the sole remaining superpower has a unique opportunity—consequent upon the historical nexus of military power, the ideology and power of globalized markets, and the emergence of an imperial state strategy of preemption—to impose itself upon the world in a way that cannot succeed but nonetheless aspires to destroy the historical truth of humanity itself and to destroy with it those modes of culture that might produce alternatives. So we hear a great deal in this book of how humanists, academic literary humanists in particular, must adopt the different temporalities of rumination, scholarship, and the longer forms to resist, expose, and displace, whenever possible, the commodified products that restrict not only civic knowledge but also human desire.

Said tells us the lesson of profound cultural changes by accounting for the differences that take place in the university and humanism's spheres of practice since the cold war. One of the most interesting parts of the book, this tale neatly exposes the profound mutual entanglement of state policy, cultural production, and commodified forms of especially nationalistic humanism. It is as if this supremely self-aware book wanted us to see that its humanist author—attuned to current realities, aware of history, and sensitive to situation—can rejustify humanism for our time by exposing linkages otherwise unseen while himself exemplifying what a humanist can yet do. And so we realize too what is at stake if the humanist Said loses: all the capacity of life, illumination, pleasure, wit, critique, and joy—all those things we so miss now—it were as if they would go out of being altogether.

It cannot be a coincidence that Said bothers himself with the late Allan Bloom, whose work lacks gravitas and interest. Bloom represents "the reemergence of what might charitably be called reductive and didactic humanism." The assertive, resentful flatulence of Bloom's complaints—"a dyspepsia of tone"—not only represents the worst reaction among those reactionary humanists of the cold war and other nationalist pasts but specifically embodies the neoconservative and more precisely the Straussian antagonism to historicism and democracy.[1] Notorious for his tasteless program to remove illicit others from university campuses—to purify the agora of those sorts of cultural collisions that fructify in their coexistence—Bloom (and his woeful followers) ridiculously assert the right, in a democratic republic, of a classically trained elite to hover above the demos and the agora.

1. Edward W. Said, *Humanism and Democratic Criticism* (New York, 2004), p. 17.

What this means is simple: the Straussian Bloom intends to make Americans accept the fact that their own immigrant, mixed, and surprising society is a failure for its perspectivism, relativism, mass culture, mass politics, voting, and liberalism. Moreover, in Said's own words, Bloom's "book seems to me to represent the nadir of what Richard Hofstadter calls anti-intellectualism in American life." For Bloom, "education ideally was to be a matter less of investigation, criticism, and humanistic enlargement of consciousness than a series of unsmiling restrictions."[2] In other words, Bloom's weak mind literalizes Strauss's worry that the U.S. is the next Weimar, a failed state suffering from the consequences of historicism, liberalism, and modernity. Of course, we know the solution: elites rule and the masses conform. Associate this aspiration to tyranny with the world-ruining power of the "sole remaining superpower," and we have a threat to humanism. As U.S. state intellectuals bray about excesses of democracy, Said convinces us that they see the very idea and fact of humans as historical beings as something to be destroyed. They do not welcome a world in which humans struggle to create and understand a world they would like to make as a place to live freely and with pleasure. Antihumanism, in this historical moment, is antidemocratic, antihistorical, and opposed to justice.

Said's book contains within it an implicit but well-staged argument against the deepest claims of Straussian neoconservatives and their allies. His remarks about the brutality of the U.S. policy of preemptive war are central to these essays revised exactly in their light. Opponents will describe the book as unpatriotic and unfair to U.S. interests, as failing to be balanced for not condemning the terrorists of 9/11. This is the position asserted by the all too aptly named Kurtz of the Hoover Institute in urging Congress to establish direct control over the teaching of foreign languages, culture, and policy—in order to suppress the supposed corrupting influence of Edward Said. Such neoconservative state intellectuals never treat history, for the simple reason that in their philosophy, history is of no matter, especially when force is available. But it is of no matter for more profound anthropological reasons. Straussians simply do not believe, as Said does, in the truth of Vico's discoveries about the historical nature of humanity or about the implicit democratic possibilities implied by human resistance to oppression and injustice in their largest as well as most quotidian efforts to make spaces of freedom. Rather, as we know from Strauss's debates with Kojève—who belongs to a tradition related to that of Auerbach and Spitzer, whom Said so much admires—he holds to a view of the species as ineffably weak, incapable of self-rule, maddeningly threatening to elites in general

---

2. Ibid., p. 18.

and philosophical wisdom in particular. So densely woven is Said's text that so seemingly small a detail as his invocation of Cola di Rienzi in a list of passionately democratic and joyous humanists—including Erasmus and Rabelais—draws in the historical details of a long human struggle. With di Rienzi's death in Rome, the last democratic national movement (enabled by the papacy) came to an end, to be replaced as a political ideal in the Italian Renaissance by the ideal of classical imperialism. The truth of that moment indicates the unique power of Vico's contribution of historicist anthropology over and against the ahistorical ambitions of imperial politics. Rienzi's defeat has a small place in Said's figural construction of the ongoing war for democratic empowerment. Early in this book, Said comes near to invoking participatory democracy as the threat the current political reaction most opposes. A Vichian anthropology, Said powerfully contends, creates not only a fuller, more interesting, and creative possibility for the human as a species that loves freedom but tightly links that historicist ambition to the multicultural, radical tradition of American democracy.

In short, the last remaining superpower is a threat to American democracy. With its end-of-history crazes and its mad impositions of "democracy" by force, it expresses its profound hatred and fear of participatory democratic possibility and has committed itself, on the foundation of capitalist commodification, to the extinction of the species as capable of thinking and living historically. It has committed itself to make the species over into something other than the human that stands at the center of high philological humanism. For if the human becomes merely the creature that consumes under the illusion that ready-made certainties and corporate totalities define reality, truth, and the limits of desire, then the very idea that the human is mind capable of understanding itself, in its own forms and those of others—the very species that lives and thinks and creates culture in that way—will no longer exist.

But Said was nothing if not committed to the power of resistance and optimism that human struggles for freedom can be achieved. Moreover, his life and this work embody the exemplary figure needed to understand how and why historicism is such a valuable science. Let's take this book as something like a novel, as it is in many ways an extended essay, in the spirit Said gave the notion years ago in reading Lukács. The essay is a form of permanent optimism in that fear of death cannot interrupt it. The paradigm of course is Socrates; life and death show that death is always external to thinking and desiring. Only death can stop his mind, but death had no place limiting the finitude of his life's project. In this book, Said produces, as he always does in his later writings, a very strong authorial voice that clearly incarnates qualities of mind and humanity that stand as an example of how interesting, how profound, how generous, and how lovingly contentious a fully human being can be. Like all good works of art, this essay tells the story that is the key to its own reading, and we are told, in clear and unmistakable terms, by precursors cast as heroic characters and others as dire but weak-minded enemies, how agonistic is life but how uniquely and importantly the humanist critic can enrich society not only by critique but by the creation of attractive, seductive, honest, and indeed heroic achievements. The speaker of this book, this Saidian voice, this accomplished work is the proof of what can be done and what is at stake in the battle waged to keep humanists who love words alive, to make them and the rest of us into humans most likely to value complexity of interest, honesty of history, and nuance in the expression of those mixed struggles that are the species life.

Throughout, the book exposes the deadly work done by veneration, hallowing, and herding. It links the rise of empire to the death of history. It castigates humanists who ignore current pressures that make them less than they might in a role that demands their best efforts at self-making and the overcoming of narrow constraints, prejudice, and ignorance. It ties the rise of apolitical professionalism to the forms of religious quietism that power requires to convince us all that its commodities stand there as if by nature.

And the book weaves other sets of words, such as that favorite of Spitzer, "situation"—which means conjunction and constellation in the spirit of astronomy—to troping and punning that allow the given of language and history to be remade by agents committed to the work needed both to preserve their own history and create objects that endure, even for those who must then correct or revise them. Details make up the book, and their weight and consequence first cause one to stop, feeling incredibly inadequate both to the admirable voice that speaks and the responsibilities it embodies and leaves to all of us. But it is never Said's effect to silence others unless they violently aim to censor or suppress. The aim rather is to overlay, to ruffle, to sting, to unsettle, and to trouble so that exciting and interesting things might result, so that imposed burdens can be rearranged and simplifications, those dangers to life and mind, can be set aside. The book stops a reader only long enough to realize its achievement and the burden it imposes as a generous invitation to join the collective effort to return the humanities to the relevant task of preserving the species that creates free life.

Resolution

Timothy Brennan

Today I am reminded again, Edward, of how much I miss your personal and intellectual presence. The U.S. government's unspeakable actions abroad are busily revealed and rationalized, exposed and explained by various media specialists. In glancing at the daily dose of doublespeak, I found my eyes drawn to the Books in Brief section of the *New York Times* featuring your latest book, *Humanism and Democratic Criticism*. After reading the review's cursory attempt to reconcile your humanism with the antihumanist assertions of the Foucault you took to task as long ago as 1975, I could not help recalling our many conversations in which you both wittily and angrily expressed your opinions about the dishonesty of that paper's coverage of the Middle East and gave vent to your dismay at being taken to be a thinker you yourself could not always recognize.

Your wit in the face of outrage is one of the qualities I admire most and will most remember about you. It is that quality so evocatively captured many years ago now (and in the context of a different but equally barbaric time) by Ernst Bloch's question, "Can hope be disappointed?"—to which Bloch's characteristic response was:

> Hope must be unconditionally disappointable, first because it is open in a forward direction, in a future-oriented direction; it does not address itself to that which already exists . . . . [And, second] because, even when concretely mediated, it can never be mediated by solid facts. For these are always, in the face of what informs hope, merely subjectively reified moments or objectively reified stoppages within a historical course of events.[1]

1. Ernst Bloch, "Can Hope Be Disappointed?" *Literary Essays*, trans. Andrew Joron (Stanford, Calif., 1998), p. 341.

That sense of hope, in other words, entails the responsibility of creating, subjectively, future facts, but also, as Bloch says, "holds *eo ipso* the condition of defeat precariously within itself." That combination is what first held my interest as we started down the road of our long friendship.

For, as you will recall, Edward, it was certainly a hopeless age, both in academic and in political terms, that first brought me into contact with you—an age in which the apparently divergent poetics of structuralism and politics of Reaganism converged. In 1980, when I barged my way into your office to get permission to enroll in your seminar on Raymond Williams and E. P. Thompson, you had not quite become a legend. *Orientalism* had appeared only two years earlier, and Columbia was still trapped in a sort of Freudian lull after the old New Criticism, defined by Lionel Trilling and carried on by Steven Marcus. But a new kind of student was just coming in to worship at the feet of an "uncircumstanced structural poetics" (as you put it a few years later). A quasi free-market exchange reigned between English and French on the second and third floors of Philosophy Hall.

Part Richard Blackmur and part Pierre Bourdieu, you were an oddity occupying the center—by breeding and charm, not just brilliance. Your lectures and conversation shifted fluidly, without apparent contradiction, among divergent registers: Leo Spitzer, Antonio Gramsci, William Appleman Williams. In retrospect, I recognize that your secret lay in being a bridge between generations. You came of age only after the first wave of post–World War II philologist emigrés from Europe and before the rather different Nietzschean and Heideggerian impulses of Continental theory took hold. Your in-betweenness might have made you either incomprehensible or a throwback, but instead you turned your interstitial status to advantage. You kept your skeptical readers off-balance.

It was a depressing time. Films like *Alien* and *Blue Collar* were giving way to Molly Ringwald and Michael J. Fox movies about twentysomething entrepreneurs. The oxygen was being pumped out of the room with programmatic brutality by individuals and organizations whose names we didn't then know but who have since crawled out into the sun (Richard Viguerie, Ralph Reed, the Scaife and Olin foundations). It amazed us to witness this transformation throughout the early 1980s, page by page, in every new issue

TIMOTHY BRENNAN is professor in the department of English and the department of cultural studies and comparative literature at the University of Minnesota. He is the author of *At Home in the World: Cosmopolitanism Now* (1997) and editor and cotranslator of Alejo Carpentier's *Music in Cuba* (2001).

of the *New York Times.* There were younger reactionaries too, not at all un-happy to leave the Vietnam War behind, attracted to Elvis Costello and The Police, who in the Ivy League trenches gave the Great Restoration a pomo edge.

Those were the times when I got to know you—as a man eager to shift the focus from the "critifacts of theory" to the atmospheric culture of a newly reassertive British, but more especially American, empire. You rec-ognized early an older insight: that the critique of society begins with the critique of religion—not simply (this time around) an emboldened right-wing Christianity, Islam, and Zionism but the Reagan era's great, two-pronged *Kulturkampf.* This dual movement was not always openly religious, but (as you were eager to show) was driven by the same impatience, the same take-no-prisoners smugness, of all antidebate mentalities: on the one side, a troglodyte rightism borrowed from the playbook of Roy Cohn and exemplified by the actor president. On the other side, hand in hand with theory's great rush from totality, the spiffy new rightism of a certain Amer-ican cultural Left, taking root in those years and exemplified later by an MLA president who achieved a little fame by slandering the victims of Gulf War syndrome and telling her organization's unemployed Ph.D.s "tough luck" while dashing off articles on Prada handbags for *Harper's Bazaar.*

As with other sediments, it took a while for all this to sink in. When I saw you on a daily basis in graduate school, I figured there must be many other Edwards out there as well. Why should other places be different? One fellow student, a British guy who later transferred to journalism, once told me, "Look around you. Is there a single professor at this place who is not neurotic? Do you want to end up that way? The only person worth staying for is Said." It was enough. Your presence made Columbia more than just another Ivy League school, more than just endowment and attitude. You took your undergrad teaching with a seriousness I found surprising, ap-plying yourself with the diligence of an untenured professor even after fame had come your way. Your grad student assistants blew your cover, telling us what books you were reading (secretly) in preparation for classes on the nineteenth-century European novel and Adorno's music criticism. That's how we knew when you were reading Chinua Achebe, Ayi Kwei Armah, and Amilcar Cabral. We caught you at it, up at 5:00 a.m. after a four-day speak-ing stint, cramming for a graduate seminar on culture and imperialism. Not that you counseled us to read the literatures of India, Africa, or Latin Amer-ica necessarily. You esteemed European (particularly English and French) literature—and your entire formation was dedicated to steeping yourself in it, reading its canons comparatively while focusing on European civilization as a common global creation. If some of us had already been introduced to

Gramsci, Adorno, and Raymond Williams, it wasn't lost on us that you were, after all, a Columbia professor who exuberantly tackled their writing, modeled your own on theirs, and blended their insights with those of grand twentieth-century scholars like Raymond Schwab or crusty misanthropic modernists like Joseph Conrad. You did all this just as the textualism of the Yale critics flourished, a contrast that symbolized your openness, freshness, and—let's face it—your courage.

I recall sitting in your living room many years later, sharing your frustration about younger generations of students. "I don't understand," you said to me. "I insult them, I coax them, I cajole them. But they all just sit there unwilling to take a stand." I remember you telling me that it was only partly because of your illness that you drifted away from teaching and took on advisees only occasionally. It is an alienation that perhaps we all feel, but how strange it must have been for you who had persuaded so many of the importance and urgency of thinking. When you asked me to come fill in for you at your seminar a few years ago, there was exasperation: "They don't debate anymore. They take everything I say as some kind of professional counsel. They just sit there." In an earlier time, the problems were very different—not the numbing effects of professionalism but frontal attacks. I am referring to those colleagues of yours from English who back in the early 1980s cornered some of us in the hall and told us, with concern, that we should refuse to study with you (for reasons clear enough, but never clearly stated).

I mentioned this earlier, but although it took me years to realize this, your great achievement in those years was to undercut the religious impulse in American intellectual life. You were worried about theory's "clubby hot-house grandeur" and its oracular model of pedagogy, fiercely evident in the 1980s but still strong today among the devotees of Gilles Deleuze, Hannah Arendt, and Antonio Negri. If the word is finally out on Leo Strauss (another emigré), who in the 1950s and 1960s taught the American Right an esoteric revanchism, steadfastly returning to an imagined Plato and Aristotle in order to create a cadre capable of advising George W. Bush on the proper conduct of World War III, one strain in literary theory was becoming, you sensed, something like a Straussianism on the Left. They nurture obscurity in quest of an elitism every bit as Nietzschean as Strauss and just as quaintly drawn to the oracles of "Greece."

Not that you responded to this challenge with the weapons of "negative reason" alone. Your writing certainly grasped the powers of Adornian critique, but you resolved to stake out a separate space, a public space, with its own feelings and its own aesthetic and political attractions. You were not always answering other critics, in other words, but creating an open-ended sense of adventure that did not depend on a foil for its identity (as did, for instance, those endless rounds of metacriticism you satirized in "Opponents, Audiences, Constituencies, and Community").[2] In the mode you chose for the essays on John Berger, Gillo Pontecorvo, Tahia Carioca, or Richard Wagner, you were neither utopian nor heterotopic. These essays were, rather, a place of conversation and sanity, antiprophetic, plebeian, and grand—*für ewig*, as Gramsci put it. You predicted, with resolve, that the religious line would be the problem of the late twentieth century and that it would pose a fight humanists could win by giving both current events and the politics of taste an intellectual prestige.

But, Edward, how quickly things are forgotten. It worries me that you have attained the status of a holy icon in postcolonial circles when many grad students have not read *Orientalism*. How many understand what you took from Vico? How many know *Orientalism* is not about imperialist literature (as one young professor recently put it) but about making thought attractive in an instrumental society of gullible spectators run by the truth managers of the fourth estate? How many really know that your essay "Traveling Theory" is not about migration but intellectual reception?[3] One can already begin to see, with your voice no longer in the halls, that your work is in danger of being consigned to the same dusty shelves as that of Raymond Williams. As you once put it about Georg Lukács in a review you wrote in the mid-1970s (just after *Beginnings*), "How is it that the militant intellectual inventor of the very conceptions of prototype, vanguard, and precursor is really nowhere to be found among contemporary critics whose watchword is prophetic avant-gardism and radical adversary intellectualism?"[4] As far as I can tell, the common view of you is that you targeted postcolonial nationalism, perceived text and history as separable categories, and read literature to show its "oppositional" content. The truth is that you provisionally defended, and were a partisan of, postcolonial nationalism in the Palestine National Committee; found textuality capable of fullness only in its historical mode; and considered literature autonomous, its politics lying not in content but in institutional function as well as in its ability to provide readers with a variable point of departure. You struggled against being absorbed by the morphological variants of the tropes of "hybridity" and "mig-

2. See Edward W. Said, "Opponents, Audiences, Constituencies, and Community," *Critical Inquiry* 9 (Sept. 1982): 1–26; rpt. in Said, *"Reflections on Exile" and Other Essays* (Cambridge, Mass., 2000), pp. 118–47.

3. See Said, "Traveling Theory," *The World, the Text, and the Critic* (Cambridge, Mass., 1983), pp. 226–47.

4. Said, "Between Chance and Determinism: Lukács's *Aesthetik*," *"Reflections on Exile" and Other Essays*, p. 63; hereafter abbreviated "BCD."

rancy" that dominated the postcolonial critical scene in the early 1990s. In fact, your term *contrapuntal criticism* was devised as an alternative to hybridity, conjuring images more of independently directed harmonizations and contacts than of mixture and mutual complicity.

As I look back now, I think we underestimated, in spite of everything, the rareness and fragility of your presence—someone who had that enviable profile and all those material advantages but who nevertheless, by temperament and conviction, held on to minority positions. Dressed in tailored suits, you still somehow managed to summon genuine indignation at the breathtaking stupidity and callousness of empire. There was something deeply informal about your formality. Every day must have been an act of translation, as if you had to say to yourself, "In these circles a minor gesture will pass for a bold sweep of the hand, so don't overdo it." But to say this perhaps makes you seem an intruder within, a sort of secret agent, and that is not what I mean to say either.

If "capturing" you has always been impossible, let me put it another way: you invented throughout the pre-*Beginnings* years at Columbia what might be called a mixed style, mimicking the European vernaculars while clearing a space for the demotic in the age of theory. I noticed over time that your speeches got simpler with age, and I took this as a sign not of waning energies brought on by illness but of an ever sharper sense of the fragility of understanding and the limits of public knowledge. You forced on yourself an inartistic art virtually unknown among your lit-crit contemporaries, which gave your published essays an openness that militated against the preciosities of craft that so clotted work taken to be serious in the profession.

What struck me very early and has remained with me since was that jovial ease you seemed to have in the company of the privileged and the powerful. Back in graduate student days, some of us made sure to live downtown to escape the dress coats and gossip of Morningside Heights. You were unbothered by it, and the campus club was in a very real sense your milieu. Remember that time in my office at Stony Brook when you came to address my seminar and we talked about Aijaz Ahmad's book (just published)? You wanted nothing more than to toss all printed copies into the incinerator. I said you were wrong to feel that way: "Look, he's driven by pique and envy, yes, and if he's mistaken about many of the facts, and if the whole book has about it an unpleasant self-interestedness, he's not wrong about those who rushed to fill the spaces you opened up without bothering to understand what you were saying about 'roads taken and not taken,' the ones who might, among deans and department heads with a superficial sense of the field, be confused with you."[5] I bring up the touchy issue of Ahmad because what

5. See Said, "Roads Taken and Not Taken in Contemporary Criticism," *The World, the Text, and the Critic,* pp. 140–57.

drove him, I think, apart from some scandalously accurate statements about the middle-class professionalism of the postcolonial critic and some real and principled differences, was that he was highly critical of you for one reason above all: your fine living. He simply could not fathom how someone could be feted and flattered and, at the same time, a problem to power.

In fact, throughout your career you embodied this very dilemma: Is it possible to be inside and outside at the same time? There is a nobility to absolute noncompliance that you could never appreciate, I think. So long as they are not of the majority (like those of the Republicans in Congress), intractable positions usually lead to ostracism. You, Edward, managed to avoid that reaction, but I was not always clear how you managed it. How did you get away with all those acerbic jabs in conversation, or in some of the more angry confrontations in print with people like Michael Walzer, Robert Griffin, and Bernard Lewis? Why didn't these remarks put you in the camp of the untouchables?

I am sure that many quietly wonder whether you didn't cheat a little by managing to live comfortably while playing the iconoclast. Maybe they are guilty of being like those critics of Lukács you once ridiculed: "One's impression was that what seemed to matter most was not Lukács's work but ... his political and moral style. The main suggestion was that, reprehensibly, he survived every difficulty" ("BCD," p. 62). There are also people who wonder whether your improbable middle road was cleared by cutting corners, stroking unsavory friends, keeping silent at opportune times to avoid unnecessary showdowns. As I understand it, that was what Ahmad thought. I realized from the start, however, even before I knew I would become an academic myself, that yours was no part-time iconoclasm—philanthropy for the sake of the tax break, as it were—but, instead, the result of discipline. It was an acrobatic performance, showing all of us how little ground is won by always sticking the truth in people's faces (a strategy that never seems to work in relationships, for instance), assuming that one's positions are so extraordinary that everyone will despise them. You didn't perceive your views to be radical (and, in fact, they were not). When living among extremists, you thought, you simply have to claim the high ground, not indulge in a counterextreme. The point is to assume the center without altering your views to approximate the reigning definition of the center. An audience has to know the range of your feelings so that you come off as neither ascetic nor saint. What often strikes me are the ways you tried to bring your full personality into your prose, all the hesitations, the asides, the admissions of defeat and intemperate hopes, the emotive or aesthetically admiring detours into passages from Dickens or Gide.

Yet another dilemma surrounding you was that you took your leads from writers like Frantz Fanon, Jonathan Swift, and Aimé Césaire, who each fashioned a voice quite unlike yours—at times brittle and nonconformist, at others pouring out in punctuated emotional outbursts before taking abrasive turns, declamatory, inquisitive, conjectural, even metaphysical. These voices disrupted the logic of relaxation, striving for discomfort—in Césaire's case, even for revelation. You, on the contrary, took the view that one moves forward by enfolding disparate views in an expansive embrace. Only in your oral performance (or, later, in your journalism) did you typically choose to slice academic propriety down the middle, separating sides to make them conscious of each other. Your many interviews, for instance, often found you caught delightfully unguarded, talking rapidly in a prose that seemed almost to outpace its object. I find your points of reference revealed better here than in any other place—the absurdities in the world of American current events, anecdotes of British imperial racism, or humorous accounts of people's agendas as revealed in personal discussions. These recorded acts of speech remain among the most penetrating parts of your "writing," which is perhaps your most decisive riposte—much more than all the sub rosa gibes against the cult of Jacques—to the opponents of logocentrism.[6]

On the whole, however, your rhetorical strategy was one of mollifying indirection. And here I register a doubt, not so much about your rhetorical strategy as about the areas of your commentary left muffled as a result; and this muffling, I think, accounts for many of the subsequent myths about your views and intentions. Given the desired impact of your work, there were two aspects that never lived up to the almost paralyzing achievement of the rest: first of all, your reluctance to work through or even directly address theories of capitalism, which would have been very different from your many confrontations in print with neoliberal governments and corporate apologists; second, your reluctance to discuss the significance of the Left Hegelian tradition or trace its intellectual influence on you and your contemporaries. That reluctance is related to, but not identical with, your vexed relationship with Marxism, which you never situated within the Left Hegelian tradition to which it clearly belongs and that informed the same European philology you extolled in *Orientalism* and elsewhere.

Despite your extraordinary understanding of the horrors and degradations of empire—for example, in *Blaming the Victims* and *The Politics of Dispossession*—and despite your admirable cantankerousness when it came to naming the culpable, you chose never to discuss capitalism systematically,

---

6. For one of his more extended engagements with deconstruction—in my opinion, his definitive one—see Said, "Criticism between Culture and System," *The World, the Text, and the Critic*, pp. 178–225.

even though there were some early gestures in this direction in the mid-1970s. We cannot explain this absence by assuming that economic modes lay beyond your scope because more than anyone you repudiated the ruses of specialization and the media's silencing of generalist critics. Admittedly, it is unpopular to speak about capitalism in so many words. One is either dismissed as a culturalist interloper or slotted off into schools of thought that have been prematurely dispatched for being ideologically passé: dependency theory, world systems theory, and so on.

In a related manner, you avoided the issue of Marxism, explaining once with great candor that the movements inspired by Marx in the Middle East—your reference point—were far from attractive: "In the whole history of Marxist organization, theory, discourse, and even practice in the Middle East, there seems to be no convincing evidence of a Marxism that went beyond Russian Marxism of the twenties and thirties." But this biographical touch notwithstanding, you carved out your position on this matter with an awareness of the American public sphere, which determined your views more than any other: "Marxism has . . . always struck me as more limiting than enabling in the current intellectual, cultural, political conjuncture" (that is, in 1992).[7] Who could argue with this? The point was even more convincing because of what you carefully remembered to add:

> It's been said about Marx that he saw this struggle as something exclusively economic; that's a serious falsification of Marx, or at least of the Hegelian residues in Marx. He was perfectly aware that the struggle was materially *expressed* and economically characterizable, but he was, I think, enormously sensitive to the shaping dialectic, to the intangible but very real figurations, to the internal unisons and dissonances the struggle produced. That is the difference between him and Hobbes, who saw life as nasty, brutish, and short."[8]

I have never called myself a Marxist either and would not consider myself one in regard to the production paradigm or the environment. But I grant (as you imply) that any educated person at this point in history is a Marxist

---

7. Said, interview by Jennifer Wicke and Michael Sprinker, in *Edward Said: A Critical Reader,* ed. Sprinker (Oxford, 1992), p. 260. He specifically addresses the expressions of Marxism within the Palestinian movement:

> Take the Popular Front, which declares itself a Marxist movement . . . . They could be described in other ways, but those of a classical Marxist party they are not. Its analyses are not Marxist. They are essentially insurrectionary and Blanquist, dispiriting to the organization of the PFLP and also 'the masses,' whom they seem to address. They have no popular base, never did. [Ibid.]

8. Said, "Interview," *Diacritics* 6 (Autumn 1976): 36.

to the degree they are also and at the same time Freudians and Darwinians. My point is that your observation can be easily reversed: not saving us from a caricature of Marx as economistic but saving us from the generally vulgar anti-Marxism—albeit not yours—that disallows the obvious need to study economics in order to be an effective cultural critic. Everything I have learned over the years in pursuit of a critique of "bad reality," as Adorno and Horkheimer characterize it, tells me that a viable theory of imperialism is impossible without studying capitalism—its historical phases, its national-cultural peculiarities, but also its unwavering constants.

I have always thought it a missed opportunity, for example, and not only in *Culture and Imperialism,* that you resisted weighing in on the question of capitalism and its materialist critique. It is true that you find the homely referent to materialities in that book by baldly reciting the scale of land accumulation by the imperial powers at their apogee (240,000 square miles of overseas territory per year). In this, you turned the literary metaphor of space into land and so moved toward an unaccommodating materialism. You saw in space an emphasis on lateral movement, on the simultaneity of life in the separate but coeval cultures of a world that exists in the present. The potency of an imperial term like *civilization,* you implied, grew out of a meeting—a confrontation in space—between cultures supposedly at different moments of development. The time that separated their savagery from our civilization was both decisive and, conveniently, unbridgeable. So your way of paying homage to the flight from idealism led you to a polemical critique of institutions, to an accusation that cast klieg lights on intellectual agents working in the press corps, corporate media, land surveys, geographic surveys, and as military occupiers of others' land. But this emphasis went forth as though, through this vehicle, one could annex the focus on the economic that, if enlisted directly, would cast you fatally into the hostile arena of "Marxism."

I wonder what might have been gained instead had you chosen to shake up your constituents. In the light of day, would it have been better or worse to have heard more clearly your insights into a tradition that so fully informed your thinking but that was so muted in your representations? You have to admit that one of the reasons so many younger scholars consider postcolonial theory to be an inaugural confrontation with Eurocentrism (when it was nothing of the sort)—and, worse, the displacement of a Marxism held to be the epitome of Eurocentrism—is that they are unfamiliar with the discourses on colonialism and imperialism that took capitalism as their starting point, work found, among other places, in Adam Smith, Jeremy Bentham, Karl Marx, Rosa Luxemburg, Georges Bataille. What strikes one, in retrospect, is how perfectly suited this tradition is to your arguments in the *Orientalism* trilogy, particularly in *Orientalism*'s final chapter on the institutions of the U.S. media as well as in *Covering Islam*. And, Edward, it strikes me as odd that, although you mention him, you had little to say about J. A. Hobson. His *Imperialism: A Study* (1902) delivers a devastating assessment of the interplay of race, religion, and morals in the employment of public tax revenues by landed capital and stock-market adventurers for the utilitarian project of subjugating "lesser peoples." All of the passion and prose elegance of philologists like Ernest Renan and Edward Lane (two of the major protagonists of *Orientalism*) are brought to bear by Hobson on a British issue in 1902 that foreshadows with depressing detail the American situation in 2002. The intellectual and political sources that made his book possible were not simply about capitalism as some austere statistical panoply or, by contrast, some monstrous epithet as large as sin but about the *culture* of capitalism.

Unlike Max Weber, Hobson's circles at the turn of the century understood culture in that vibrant, holistic sense reminiscent of the best political economy: as a dynamic web of forces produced by baleful policies that are both individually chosen and systemic. Hobson's writing harmonized with rough contemporaries who were equally relevant to *Culture and Imperialism*'s themes of literary complicity and who, in turn, directly challenged that book's claim that anti-imperial projects among European and North American intellectuals were relatively recent. Foregrounding the problem of capitalism would have allowed you to leave, along with so much else, an indelible picture of those literary intellectuals who, unlike Austen or Trollope, entered the economic fray: Leonard Woolf in *Imperialism and Civilization* (1928), William Morris in *News from Nowhere* (1891), and R. B. Cunninghame Graham in *The Imperial Kailyard* (1896). It would have fed your thesis elsewhere that so much of theory unwittingly repeats its repressed precursors.

On a related issue, I would like to bring up the *Diacritics* interview of 1976, in which you mention "dialectics." How rare that gesture was for you! Not unheard of, just rare—although less rare than your acolytes seem to believe. You drew so often on Williams, Gramsci, Lukács, Fanon, Emile Habiby, Joseph Needham, and (above all) Adorno that one had a right to expect you would deal squarely with dialectical thought and the Hegelian tradition. Your forte was always the capacious elaboration of ideas, the stating of ideas in the air yet unexpressed, but here, when it came to dealing with the same Hegelian tradition that so affected your thinking, there was relative silence broken only by transitory comments in book reviews. Nonetheless, as early as 1966—a formative time in your career—we find you drawn, in your very first published piece, to the work of Lucien Goldmann, whose argument "stands in the center of a highly challenging and flowing pattern, a 'dialectic' whose every detail sustains and is sustained by every other detail."[9] It is altogether clear that many of your most insistent motifs—among them, your repudiation of the phenomenologists' "lonely ego," the "rigorous intellectual effort" that forms the "inner coherence" of an author's work, the value of "historical consciousness"—are all emergent precisely here. At this moment, in the presence of the dialectical tradition, which you deliberately connect to *"les sciences humaines"* of Dilthey, Vico, and Auerbach, you establish your own continuity of thinking with Marxism ("SM," pp. 448, 447, 445, 444). What excites you about Goldmann's effort, among other things, is the theory it posits of the way "in which individual parts can be said to make up a whole greater than a mere sum of its parts"—a view, you argue, that leads away from a monadic consciousness to a relational "group consciousness," which is not simply Hegelian but philological ("SM," p. 444).

It is a point probably lost on those who already "know" you to be the founder of postcolonial theory's politics of discursivity, but recall the way you put the matter of dialectics on the eve of *Orientalism's* appearance almost a decade later in 1975:

> I have a great deal of sympathy for what [Marxist groups within the MLA] are trying to do, but I think it is a fundamental misjudgment of reality to base one's political work on an unsituated effort to show that Marxism is principally a reading technique . . . . What I am saying is that . . . . to turn a literary or intellectual project immediately into a political one is to try to do something quite undialectical. But to accept the form of action prescribed in advance by one's professional status—which in the system of things is institutionalized marginality—is to restrict oneself politically and in advance.[10]

Interestingly, it is also to Goldmann that you returned, almost a decade later, in "Traveling Theory," in an effort to translate the meaning of dialectics, colloquially put, by way of analyzing what you call the "tamings" of reading over time as texts pass from one to another social circumstance—in this case how the concepts of reification and totality passed from Lukács to Goldmann to Williams and Foucault.[11] And again dialectics reasserts itself in your thinking in the mid-1970s, just as you are finishing *Orientalism*, in a review of Béla Királyfalvi's study of Lukács's *Aesthetik*, where you con-

---

9. Said, "A Sociology of Mind," review of *The Hidden God: A Study of Tragic Vision in the "Pensées" of Pascal and the Tragedies of Racine*, by Lucien Goldmann, *Partisan Review* 33 (Summer 1966): 444; hereafter abbreviated "SM."

10. Said, "Interview," p. 39.

11. See Said, "Traveling Theory," p. 238.

sider the Hungarian's logic to be "Hegelian in its dynamism, but more radical . . . in its thrust into totality" ("BCD," p. 67). But you never exalted the lineage by name, and you resisted being identified with it—strategically perhaps, but thereby leaving your thoughts to the interstitial comments of a long-term dialogue. Your reliance on it, though, cannot be in doubt. Just before your death, you again acknowledged, more clearly than before, that the work of Auerbach, one of your most obvious intellectual sources, "arose from the themes and methods of German intellectual history and philology; it would be conceivable in no other tradition than in that of German romanticism and Hegel."[12]

I miss your occasional calls, the meetings for drinks in New York, the latest in *Al-Ahram*. I would have liked to prod you more about a different Gramsci—the one who liked to talk about a "conformism from below"— a feeling for which Williams seems to have based his early work in adult education or (in a much more mediated and aesthetic sense) that one finds in Mikhail Bakhtin's writing on transgressive laughter and grotesque realism, the raucous power and grace of lower-class humanity. But one can't have it all. You are gone, and no literary device is going to change that. There are no longer any conversations with you, just with others through you. We are left only with that "interpretive circle" you once wrote about in Goldmann—that moment when "man faces and is faced by, interprets and is interpreted by, his works" ("SM," p. 448). And yet, Edward, I have tried to imagine this conversation with you today, in part to remind myself of the lecture you gave in Minneapolis a couple of years ago on "late style." Some critical work is special, you argued, "not as harmony and resolution, but as intransigence, difficulty, and unresolved contradiction."[13]

12. Said, "Introduction to the Fiftieth Anniversary Edition," in Erich Auerbach, *Mimesis: The Representation of Reality in Western Literature,* trans. Willard R. Trask (Princeton, N.J., 2003), p. xii.

13. Said, "Late Style: Adorno, Lampedusa, Cavafy," lecture, University of Minnesota, Minneapolis, 22 Feb. 1999.

Homi Bhabha Talks with Noam Chomsky

Noam Chomsky

The Palestinian Past

HOMI BHABHA: Did you have many conversations with Edward Said? I mean, did you participate in any conferences or the like, and can you recall something of the feelings between you?

NOAM CHOMSKY: Edward Said and I were very close friends, but like most of my friends I barely see them, we're just too busy. So I didn't see Edward a lot, we didn't meet frequently. But we met often enough, and in interesting situations, and some of them were ones nobody ever talked about. It started in the late 1970s. Edward became very much concerned about the direction the PLO was taking. Which was highly self-destructive. In fact, it was the most self-destructive national liberation movement I've had anything to do with, and I've had to do with plenty of them. But I think partly it was they were coming out of some kind of a feudal background, which made them incapable of understanding the way a democratic society works. Every Third World movement, I mean even the North Koreans, crazy as they are, recognized that they better try to develop some support in the United States, otherwise they were in deep trouble. I mean, you can't look at the world and not understand that. The only ones who *never* understood it were the PLO. And for them it would have been easier than anyone else. I mean, if Arafat, Farouq Qadooni, and the rest of them had showed up in the 1970s, telling people the truth, the truth being I'm a conservative nationalist and I'd like to get elected mayor in my own city so I can rip people off and put the money in the bank. [Laughing.] And our own people would like to be able to elect their own mayors—which happened to be the truth. If they had come and told that to people, they would have been extremely popular and everyone would have said, yes, that makes perfect sense, we'll support you. They wouldn't. What they had to do was come with a Kalashnikov, pretending to be Marxist revolutionaries, of which they understood not a word. And, in fact, you know, they brag about the fact that they're recognized by the Fiji Islands, so on and so forth. Of course, that just alienates people. And this was going on constantly, made it extremely hard to develop the kinds of solidarity movements that did develop and were effective in Indochina and in Central America and, finally, East Timor, and places like that. They just couldn't do it. And sometimes it was outlandish. Edward was involved seriously in trying to change this. Just to give you an illustration. At the time of the 1982 invasion of Lebanon, one of the most distinguished figures in the Israeli military, one of the founders of the army, a very honest man, incidentally, a person of really great integrity and honor, when he went to Lebanon he was too old to fight in the war, but he went as a civil advisor or something. And he was appalled by what the Israeli army was doing. He wrote a book in Hebrew called—it translates as *War Diary,* which was just his diary describing what was done. Well. I asked a small press here, South End Press, if they would agree to publish it and the translation of it, and we got somebody to translate it, and they were going to do it, but they didn't have any resources. I asked Edward to see if he could get the PLO—and not to subsidize it—but just to help in the distribution, to buy copies and put them in libraries and things like that because otherwise nobody would ever see it. But they didn't do it. They answered him back that they would do it only if it said, stamped on the front, "Published with the support of the PLO." You know what that's going to do with a book. But this conception that you somehow have to reach out to all, you have to reach out—they would never understand that. Edward tried to change that. We had meetings, which I don't think would have been discussed, around the late seventies or the early eighties, people who were highly sympathetic to the Palestinians, but then critical of the PLO. I recall meetings when the PLO delegation came to the UN; Edward arranged for us to have private meetings. I mean their conception of politics is a meeting in a back room with Henry Kissinger working out some kind of a deal, and that's not the way it works in a democratic so-

NOAM CHOMSKY is Institute Professor (retired) at the Massachusetts Institute of Technology where he has been on the faculty since 1955. He has written and lectured widely on linguistics, philosophy, intellectual history, and international affairs. Among his recent books are *Middle East Illusions* and *Hegemony or Survival.*

ciety. You have to have popular support, and it will ultimately influence government policy. If you're talking to Henry Kissinger or, you know, George Shultz in the back room, they're going to be representing their interests, not your interests.

Binational State

HB: What do you think of Edward's desire for a binational state, which seemed to be at once utopian and utterly necessary?

NC: I was writing about this from 1967 up till 1973, writing extensively, and I think, at that time, it was a sensible idea. After the Israeli conquest of the territories, Israel was in a position to basically settle the problem. By 1971, Egypt was offering a full peace treaty and offered nothing to the Palestinians. Jordan was willing to settle, a full peace treaty, and Israel understood that. They knew these were genuine peace offers. They rejected them because they wanted to expand into Sinai.

But suppose they had accepted the Egyptian offer, which essentially would have ended the interstate conflict, and, of course, accepted Jordan's offer. Well, then they would have been left with the West Bank. What should they have done? Well, in my opinion, what they should have done, from their own point of view, was to establish a federal system in cis-Jordan with a Jewish-based area and a Palestinian-based area. It just makes no sense to break that region up into two worlds. All you have to do is travel around it. Because of the border, it wouldn't make any sense. They are integrated in all kinds of ways. Any Jewish state or Palestinian state is going to be discriminatory, just like any Christian state or, you know, white state or anything else. That's, more or less, unavoidable, but you can attenuate the discriminatory character by federal integration.

And over time, as other forms of connections and as people develop—after all, we're not just Jews and Palestinians; there are class relations, intellectual relations, professional relations, as further circumstances permit—you can end up with closer integration. Well, at that time, it was a very sensible proposal and it would have saved plenty of misery and turmoil—if it had been carried out, but you couldn't, nobody knew how. No Palestinians wanted to hear it. No Israeli wanted to hear it. It was a mess. I did write about it a lot. It's one of the reasons why I'm so hated. By 1973, it was finished. So that once the U.S. and Israel refused to accept Sadat's offer it virtually compelled Sadat to go to war. After the war, even Kissinger understood that you can't just dismiss the Egyptians. He doesn't understand much, but he understands force. And the Egyptians said, "Look, we're not a basket case, so we can't be dismissed." And at that point the United States moved towards what ultimately was the

Camp David agreements, which essentially accepted Sadat's 1971 offer. Now that's presented in the United States as a dramatic triumph. It's, in fact, a diplomatic catastrophe. By rejecting the offer in 1971, they created a situation where there was a terrible war, a lot of suffering, even a nuclear alert. And then, finally, they came around accepting something like Sadat's original offer. Of course, you can't say that. So you have to present it differently. However, by the mid-seventies, the issue of a binational federal state was gone because by that time the international consensus had taken shape for the first time, and it was taking shape around the two-state settlement. In January of 1976, there was a Security Council resolution on it, which the U.S. vetoed and from then on the issue was a two-state settlement. Personally, I thought it was a bad idea, but, given that there was no alternative, I went along with it, too. The possibility of a binational federal system was essentially gone.

I talked to Edward about it a lot. He was strongly in favor of the two-state settlement, and I couldn't disagree with him, given the possibilities. In fact, we agreed about that completely. As for the Oslo process, Edward and I thought the same things. It was a complete sellout on Arafat's part, it was perfectly obvious. Palestinians couldn't see it. In fact, right after, just to show how extreme it was, right after the Oslo agreement was signed in September 1993, I actually wrote about it right away; I said it was a total sellout. But there was a meeting here at MIT that included a leading Palestinian. I can't identify him. But he was from Israel and a Palestinian, a friend, a personal friend. We talked at the meeting and I said what I thought. And we went out for coffee afterwards, and he told me he didn't disagree but that if I tried to say that on the streets of Ramallah I'd be lynched because they wanted desperately to believe the Oslo agreement. It's not uncommon, you know; people who are really suffering want to have hope. And even when they're being kicked in the face, they prefer to believe something else. And the truth is hard to face. But the truth was it was a complete sellout. Arafat undermined the genuine authentic Palestinian leadership, which had been negotiating in Washington, but refused to give up on the issue of the settlements.

The Right of Return
HB: And the right to return issue?
NC: And the issue of the refugees—here I strongly disagree with my Palestinian friends, close friends. I have felt for years and I've been trying to tell them for years something very unpopular: you cannot hold out false hopes in front of the refugees. The people who are suffering miserably in refugee camps in Lebanon, it's just not honest and not moral to tell them

you have hope of returning to your homes because they don't. First of all, there is no international support for it. And under the unimaginable circumstances that there would be international support, Israel would use the ultimate weapon to prevent it, even if that required using lethal weapons to blow up their region. What they used to call the Samson complex back from the 1950s. If they were forced to accept the bringing of the Palestinians back, they would prevent it by any means possible. But, furthermore, the issue is not going to arise because there's never going to be any support for it. You know, they could be assimilated, but it's meaningless, it's just not going to happen, and we know it's not going to happen. Now it could happen over a course of evolution through two states, integrating them, federal, you know, moving on to some new state. Then, it could possibly happen, but it can't be part of the short-term settlement. I must say I disagree with almost all of my friends on this. I mean, opposing the Geneva accords on those grounds, I don't think makes sense. In fact, you can kind of trace it. At the time of the Taba negotiations in January of 2001, there was a considerable improvement over Camp David, considerable, not enough, but considerable. The Geneva accords is a bigger improvement. The Taba negotiations were never continued. I mean they were continued sub rosa, the Geneva accords, but not openly. They were blocked, Sharon was elected. It was easy for him to block them because of the suicide bombings. You know, people are driven to desperation, to make and say terrible things. But, as a tactic, it was senseless. And I've been saying this for thirty-five years. The first article—one of the first articles I wrote was actually for a Palestinian audience, around 1969—basically told my Palestinian friends that the PLO tactics are senseless. If you carry out acts that are unacceptable on moral grounds to any decent person, you're not going to get any support, and you shouldn't get any support. First of all, it was morally outrageous, and it was politically idiotic. I mean Israel was moving to the borders. It was pushing to the borders the Mizrahim—you know, the Jews from the Arab countries, and they were poor working-class people. Those are the ones the PLO carried out the terror on. What kind of political idiocy, apart from any moral level, is it to attack poor Jews from the Arab countries and kill them? That's going to win you some support somewhere?

A Hopeful Future

HB: Finally, do you see a cadre of more positive leadership, more moral leadership on the Palestinian side?

NC: Very good people, the people who were Edward's friends, like . . .

HB: Barghouthi. And will they be able to break through? What are the conditions? Just one or two things that would allow them to actually break through and carry popular solidarity on both sides?

NC: Well, they have to work in their own communities. But what is lacking and what is crucial is anything in the United States. Like, when the intifada began. Let me just give you an explicit incident to show how it really works in many cases. When this second intifada began, the first few days, actually the first month of the intifada, the killing ratio was twenty to one, twenty Palestinians to one Jew. And they were Israeli soldiers. Nobody cared about it here. As long as it was twenty to one, who cares? When it got down to three to one, it became a tragedy. But the first couple of days of the intifada, Israel was using helicopters—meaning American helicopters, they don't make them—to attack civilian targets, killing and wounding dozens of people. It was actually being reported. After three days of the intifada, on October third, Clinton made the biggest deal in a decade to send new military helicopters to Israel. Right at the very moment when these helicopters were being used to attack, murderously to attack civilian targets. It wasn't reported here. A couple of us tried very hard to get it reported. Actually, I went to the offices of the *Boston Globe* with a group of people to try to convince the editors to just publish the facts. You don't have to say anything about it, just allow it to appear in public. It was in the Israeli press and it was in the international press. It was on international wires. So, as long as the United States stands in the way, there will be no political settlement. Its force is just far too great. And unless there's some kind of a solidarity movement here, say, let's take some of these nonviolent resistance actions going on right at this moment, they could succeed. You know, they could be the basis for a settlement. But not if they're totally blocked here.

The Turn

Ranajit Guha

In *The Question of Palestine* (1979) Edward Said speaks of 1967 as "a watershed year" for his people. The occupation of the West Bank and Gaza by Israel helped to crystallize their sense of a common Palestinian identity grounded in the bitterness of dispossession. Years later he would describe himself in his memoir as "no longer the same person after 1967." A carefree wanderer until then he was seized, like his compatriots, by the anguish of displacement. For the first thirty years of his life he had moved from home to home, school to school, and to some extent job to job, commuting between cultures and communities in several countries and two continents. Cosmopolitan itinerancy doesn't seem to have worried him too much. In fact, his recollection of those days leaves little doubt that he enjoyed the open and expansive life not cast in concrete at any particular site. But the events of 1967 changed all that and made him realize, as never before, that once he had a home to call his own, but was homeless now. This loss, the latest in a series of dislocations suffered by his family and relatives, was assimilated to "the dislocation that subsumed all other losses," namely, the loss of Palestine. Henceforth this would be a point for time and place to intersect in his work and coordinate a many-sided engagement with literature, history, and politics in some of the most memorable reflections on the human predicament.

That predicament acquires a particularly high profile in the figure of the exile in nearly all his accounts of Palestine. Indeed it is central to the existential concern that aligns each of these narratives in an unmistakable kinship with his literary essays. It is as if the dissonance of life calls for a new dialogue between life and literature in the light of the experience of exile, and Said responds by setting up such a dialogue in his studies of the novel that, as Lukács has argued, owes its form to that very dissonance. This is clearly brought out, albeit on the limited scale of the short story, in his reading of Conrad's "Amy Foster" and his use of fiction to make sense of displacement as a significant fact of modern life.

It is the story of a shipwreck. The boat, packed with migrants lured by the prospect of jobs and gold, was on its way to America when it sank off the coast of England. One of the passengers, a poor villager called Yanko Goorall from eastern Europe, was lucky enough to be still alive as the storm dumped him on the beach. The locals made him feel positively unwanted. However, he managed to find some work and a place to live, and eventually, we are told, the villagers "became used to seeing him" even if "they never became used to him." What made him unacceptable was his foreignness, expressed in the way he dressed, walked, sang, talked, or recited the Lord's Prayer—in everything that stood for language, broadly speaking. In the absence of verbal contact with the natives and with nobody around to converse with in his own mother tongue, the young castaway was trapped in an inescapable loneliness.

The only chink in the gloom was a relationship that developed between him and Amy Foster, a village girl, who had been attracted to him at first sight, treated him with much sympathy and kindness, and helped him at least partly to break out of his isolation. They defied local opinion to get married. A child was born. All seemed set for a happy ending when he fell seriously ill. Amy, who had been his only refuge so far from the incomprehensibility that had cut him off from the rest of the population, was now affected by it herself. The failure of communication between them became so intense that she could not bear it anymore and walked out with the baby, leaving him to die unattended and alone.

It is well known that this story has acquired a particular salience in Said's work on exile. Thus in his essay "Reflections on Exile" (1984) he uses it to suggest (as he does elsewhere as well) that Conrad's own sense of alienation led him to identify himself with the castaway and make the problem of communication central to his plot. The consequence, in Said's opinion, has been not only to exaggerate the misunderstanding between Amy and Yanko but fashion "this neurotic exile's fear" into an "aesthetic principle" and romanticize his death. However, when he returns to the text nearly fifteen years later in his essay "Between Worlds" (1998), there is a remarkable change of

RANAJIT GUHA held various research and teaching positions in India, England, the United States, and Australia before his retirement in 1988. He is the founding editor of *Subaltern Studies* and the author of *A Rule of Property for Bengal* and *Elementary Aspects of Peasant Insurgency in Colonial India.*

tone, striking for the absence of any imputation of romanticism whatsoever. On the contrary, Conrad is appreciated without reserve for his portrayal of the exile's sense of "loss of home and language in the new setting"
as a loss that is "irredeemable, relentlessly anguished, raw, untreatable,
always acute." Not a hint of sentimentality here. It is the "severity" of representation that impresses Said.

What is no less significant is that he unhesitatingly takes his cue from
this very Conradian idea and sets out to write a moving account of his sense
of "loss of home and language" in the rest of the essay. Among other things,
he speaks ruefully about the consequence of settling down to a tenure in
the academic profession in America "as a way of submerging my difficult
and unassimilable past" and the growing realization that he had thereby
accommodated himself to "the exigencies of life in the U.S. melting-pot"
almost to the point of having his past "annulled." This, as Adorno had
warned, was the fate of the migrant intellectual. So, with very little time left
to him, says Said, he began to take stock of his past and "once again I recognized that Conrad had been there before me."

This recognition is curious, to say the least. For in his reading of "Amy
Foster" and elsewhere, he had been keen so far to distance himself from
Conrad on one critical issue. He did not like the portrayal of the exile as a
much misunderstood romantic hero, which is how he read it and believed
it to have been induced by the author's self-identification with the fate of
those wretched figments of his imagination. But now his judgement tilts
favorably to highlight Conrad's stubborn refusal to allow exilic pressures to
empty his past of its content. In the light of this resistance, as documented
by Said himself, it would appear that Conrad had indeed been fairly realistic
in his depiction of the exile as a victim of those very pressures. Said, of
course, does not acknowledge this in so many words. He simply identifies
himself with Conrad's predicament just as the latter had done with the
exile's. Nevertheless, the shift, which amounts to a significant turn, catches
the reader unawares and prompts him to ask what brought it about.

Whether Said had himself noticed any such turn in his thinking is not
clear. However, we have in his writings all we need for an answer to our
question. The first thing to notice is that this particular shift is not the kind
caused by the 1967 war. Said refers to that earlier moment again and again
as a historical benchmark in the life of his people. It was then that they
stepped out of "the conventional Arab set-up" in which they had been contained for decades and began to assert a distinctly "Palestinian self-help,
self-responsibility, self-identity in the form of consensus political organizations." No longer just refugees, "the exiled Palestinians became a political
force of estimable significance."

Said, too, closed ranks with them to assume the role for which he came to be known as perhaps the most eloquent advocate of the Palestinian cause abroad. Far from being the passive onlooker that he had been so far, he now became a participant in the resurgent nationalist movement. Like his compatriots, he too was fired by the hope of the dispossessed to return to the lost homeland and their determination to act together accordingly. It was a forward-looking vision with no room in it for the exile as an individual trapped in loneliness and isolation. If at all, he would figure in it merely as an irrelevant entity liable to be regarded by the activist as somewhat unreal and romanticized.

This perhaps was the image Said saw in Conrad's castaway in 1984—an image of utter dejection that looked so pathetically small and inconsequential in the background of a rising collective enthusiasm. But there is a serious problem with this view. It does not take into account the fact that the perspective of hope mentioned above is not available to the exile marooned, like Yanko Goorall, in an alien community. Unlike the mass of the dispossessed he does not have an inexhaustible fund of ressentiment to provide him with the will and energy to fight his way out of misfortune. The latter is entirely of his own making—a failure of judgement on his own part involving an overestimation of his capacity to cope with the risks of his adventure. He has no one else to blame other than himself. Nor does he belong to a collectivity on which he can rely for support or solace in his distress. For he has drifted too far away alas from his people and the distance grows with time.

That distance means a loss to him for which there is no parallel in the condition of those displaced en masse by the violence of invasion or occupation. The loss of homeland does not amount, in their case, to loss of contact with their own community of native speakers. If anything, the impact of a shared adversity may even have some sealing effect on the linguistic bond between them and inspire songs of courage and joy to celebrate their engagement in a common struggle. In fact, Said draws our attention to much the same sort of development in contemporary Palestinian literature.

By contrast, the exile like Yanko has no possibility at all of communicating in his mother tongue. Entirely on his own among people who are not only unfamiliar with but hostile to anything that remotely sounds like it, he is without any means of interlocution whatsoever. There is therefore nothing he can do to break out of the silence and despair in which he is virtually immured. Condemned to a living death, he may indeed end up in a "solitary death illuminated by unresponsive, uncommunicating eyes." This is the other register of exilic predicament, the staple of Conradian fiction, for which Said does not seem to have made any allowance in his earlier interpretation.

Eventually, seven years later, he did change registers. This occurred in

1991 when, as he was to recall it in the essay "Between Worlds," medical diagnosis "suddenly revealed to me the mortality I should have known about before . . . and I found myself trying to make sense of my own life as its end seemed alarmingly nearer." Conrad's view of the castaway's death was to appear to him now in a new light—the darker light of another depth characterized by the narrator in "Amy Foster" as a tragedy. Not the familiar classical Greek kind, it was one of "'a subtler poignancy'" generated, he said, as much by "'irreconcilable differences'" as by "'that fear of the Incomprehensible that hangs over all our heads—over all our heads.'" The "irreconcilable differences" in this formulation are easily recognized as what isolated and finally killed Yanko Goorall. But what does "the Incomprehensible" stand for? As a fear "that hangs over all our heads," with the last four words reiterated for emphasis, it is obviously not limited to exiles alone, but extends to all human beings. The only threat that applies to all of them without exception is of course death.

Paradoxically, it is "the Incomprehensible" that prompts Said, too, to try and make sense of his own life. It is not the first time that he does so under an external stimulus. The 1967 war had led to such a review of his own past culminating in his identification with the dispossessed Palestinians in their agony and their struggle. It was, on his part, an attempt at self-realization on the public register of exilic experience. But the exile that the intimation of mortality revealed now as the hitherto unexamined self was of a different kind altogether. It had more in common with Conrad, and Said, as he looked back on his life in the light of the new knowledge, pointed to that existential affinity by saying: "Once again I recognized that Conrad had been there before me." This helps no doubt to clarify all of what he meant except for that single phrase, "once again." What are we to make of it when we know how decisive he has been so far in his judgment that Conrad was led by his own fear of a solitary death to grossly exaggerate the extent and intensity of the exile's isolation?

Evidently, there is some ambiguity here. It is not difficult to understand why. For the statement belongs to a period of deep introspection immediately following the diagnosis of his illness. As we have it from Said himself, it started with a letter addressed to his dead mother and culminated three years later in the work that would eventually shape up as his autobiography. The words that connect him with Conrad as his predecessor come somewhere between these two poles of atavism and confession. Who knows what the traveller condemned to the certainty of a fast-approaching death sees in that region of light and shade, and what fugitive patterns catch his eye only to be lost in the gathering darkness?

As one of those patterns formed in such obscurity, Said's self-identification with Conrad may not be directly intelligible. But it does make sense if read in the context of what he has to say about the convergence of his own experience and Conrad's. This relates to the latter's narrative practice. Conrad, as a storyteller, often chose a narrator, such as Kennedy in "Amy Foster," to do the talking for him when it concerned a tale of exile. It was as if he needed someone else and indirect utterance to act as a buffer between him as an exile and the death to which his characters were foredoomed as victims of failure in human communication. A perfectly self-conscious strategy, it was a way of writing creatively to defer death in the full knowledge of its certainty.

Said seems to have this in mind when he recalls how for years his critical engagement with Conrad had been like "a steady groundbass" to which much that he experienced was set in counterpoint. But that was done, as he put it, working "through the writings of other people," that is, intuitively and without self-knowledge. This set it apart from Conrad's storytelling mediated by the narrator's voice. For self-knowledge was indeed what enabled the great master to play the endgame on his own terms fully aware that he was going to lose, but that his loss would not be such as to make death so proud. Said, too, sets out to know himself, "trying," as he says, "to make sense of my own life as its end seemed alarmingly nearer." It was the conscious acknowledgment of an impending end that enabled him to see more clearly than ever before how his own experience of exile converged with Conrad's. What the writer and the critic, one as homeless as the other, shared was their refusal, articulated by each in his own way, to compromise with the deadly power of alienation and incomprehensibility over minds and cultures. Ironically it took the knowledge of death and its terrible lucidity to enable these two streams of life-enhancing experience to converge.

Conjunctural Traces: Said's "Inventory"

Harry Harootunian

In the *Prison Notebooks* Gramsci says: "The starting-point of critical elaboration is the consciousness of what one really is, and is 'knowing oneself' as a product of the historical process to date, which has deposited in you an infinity of traces, without leaving an inventory."

—Edward Said, *Orientalism*[1]

What appears to have been an official mourning period following the death of Edward Said is over, a death the magnitude of which managed to proliferate numerous services around the country and even enlist celebrities and generate a professional class of mourners on occasion. It is now time to revisit his diverse achievements and begin the task of reassessing their meaning for the scene of humanist disciplines and contemporary political intervention. Said's death puts an end to an energetic activity motivated by the necessity of always keeping alive the tense but asymmetrical relationship between culture and politics and the almost impossible task of resisting the temptation, at least for American academics, of slipping into the former as if it were a more than adequate substitute for the latter. In fact, I've always felt that his writings, ranging from elevated forays into classical music to the everyday politics of the Palestinian quest for national independence, must have created an insurmountable tension that challenged and threatened the limit of his capacity to withstand stress. Max Weber went into involuntary hibernation for five years because of nervous exhaustion caused by his intellectual labors, even though he confessed that he wanted to know how much he could bear. Although Weber was intensely interested in the new Weimar constitution and deeply involved in realizing its republican prospects for Germany after World War I, his political concerns, I suspect, were not just simply different from those that had captured Said's attention but probably less stressful. Unlike Said, Weber was not dogged by a commitment to politics that either contradicted or clashed with his cultural pieties. With Said there was, I believe, the ceaseless attempt to juggle the world

---

1. Edward W. Said, *Orientalism* (New York, 1978), p. 25; hereafter abbreviated *O*.

of high and often airless literary criticism with the polemics demanded by the daily struggle, the often uneven and unstable relationship between his own self-acknowledged calling of cultural critique and the desire for concrete political practice, one that seemed always mediated by his own concern for a politics of representation—culture—and a representation of politics occasioned by Palestinian national aspirations, forming the figure of an arabesque of entanglement of history and contingency. While Said flirted with forms of Marxism as a fellow traveler among what we might call the league of internationalist nationalists (Frantz Fanon, Amilcar Cabral, C. L. R. James, Takeuchi Yoshimi), he early separated his project from it precisely because of an absence of a "continuous native Marxist . . . culture" to back up literary culture and its distance from "concrete political struggle."[2] This observation undoubtedly explains not only why Said appealed to heavyweights of high culture and literary criticism like Arnold, Auerbach, Spitzer, and Curtius and the cultural empowerment they embodied for him but also why he insistently maintained a steady passion for national political struggle at arm's length from this lofty, European vista.

In the case of Erich Auerbach, we have to wonder what exactly Said had in mind in embracing a scholarly figure who spent the wartime in Turkey, once regarded the threshold of Asia and the classical boundary marking off the "Orient" from Europe, obsessively fixed on writing an account of realist representation of the West that both reinforced the claims of cultural unity that Said's *Orientalism* sought to repudiate and quite purposefully seemed to have bracketed out the immediate environment in order to produce the text in question, *Mimesis*. Said was aware of the alienating effect of Auerbach's exilic existence in Turkey and his (geographic) distance from the very cultural unity he was trying to recuperate. If Auerbach briefly acknowledged the constrained circumstances under which he wrote *Mimesis* it was the philologist who complained that he did not have the proper scholarly materials and tools available to him in Istanbul and that he could not have

---

2. Said, "Reflections on American 'Left' Literary Criticism," *The World, the Text, and the Critic* (Cambridge, Mass., 1983), p. 166. See also Michael Denning, *Culture in the Age of the Three Worlds* (London, 2004), pp. 187-88. In *Orientalism*, Said had already argued that "American Marxist theorists in particular, have avoided the effort of seriously bridging the gap between the superstructural and the base levels in textual, historical scholarship" (*O*, p. 13).

HARRY HAROOTUNIAN is professor of East Asian studies and history at New York University. His most recent work is titled *The Empire's New Clothes: Paradigm Lost and Regained* (2004), and he is coediting with Hyun Ok Park a special issue for *Boundary 2* called "Problems of Comparability/Possibilities for Comparative Studies" (2005).

written such a book had he still resided in Europe. In this confession, Said recognized that Auerbach's exile from the culture he was dedicated to reaffirming called attention to nation and home, being "at home in a place" and belonging to it. Auerbach's allegiance to the culture of place from which he was now estranged explains the intensity of his desire to restore to it the unity he would never have recognized had he remained in Europe. While this declaration may seem to have answered the question of Said's commitment to culture, which he envisaged as an environment in which individuals and their work were located and embedded—their world—it falls short of explaining the manifestly asymmetrical mix of culture and politics he, in contrast to Auerbach, had embraced. For Auerbach, Turkey simply constituted the refuge of exile and offered a culture to which he neither belonged nor in which he had any really abiding interest (unlike Said's relationship to the U.S.). In fact, its very absence in his text and the negativity he associated with it (poor libraries) underscore the importance of his cultural act to rethink the unity of Europe's cultural tradition and to authenticate a singular identity between its origins and its modern present. Although Said was educated and trained in the tradition upheld by Auerbach, its cultural environment clashed spectacularly with a politics of Palestinian national liberation, with its own cultural claims that projected yet another vision and version of home and environment and a future prospect of belonging to it. In Auerbach's cultural act it is possible to detect the specter of actualizing a different kind of politics of conservation and return rather than transformation. Said would continue throughout his career to share with him his sympathy for nation and heritage and the culture it signified, but not exactly the politics of restoration associated with it. Yet the removed and "Oriental" perspective enabling Auerbach to reconfigure Europe's apparent lost unity as the condition for reaffirming the place to which he belonged (physically and spiritually) was vastly different from the remoteness Said often summoned to describe his world and project for it. While Said was an interpreter (and often self-appointed custodian) of the tradition Auerbach rescued in his Turkish exile, his own politics of Palestinian liberation belonged to an altogether different register that could only repudiate, or be repudiated by, its cultural conceits. (One could also certainly speculate what his particular political passion would have meant for his favored theorists of high culture.)

In this regard, Said's lifelong identification with Auerbach often worked against his best impulses. His acceptance of the fantasy figure of a unified cultural tradition explains why he was always so reluctant to eliminate the idea of a unified West from his own discourse even though dismantling its claims was at the heart of his critical project; and his decision to embody the cultural self-satisfaction of bourgeois Europe with the politics of Palestinian national liberation—a colonial struggle—produced a curious coupling that could only collide with Gramsci's understanding of culture and politics to the point that he—Said—would hold back from fully accepting the Marxism that informed it. It was, after all, Gramsci who early saw the filiation between forms of cultural expression and political action and who subsequently envisaged a program devoted to figuring cultural production as a mode of political struggle. With this move Gramsci managed to envisage another kind of environment of belonging occupied by the historical common sense of the people now actualized in a conjunctural and daily struggle with the forces of hegemony and coercion to disclose a discrepancy between culture and politics. It was this discrepancy Said recognized in his cultural-political practice and even tried (as I will show later) to utilize. What he overlooked was a discrepancy of politics and culture that constituted the real site of conjunctural struggle rather than one that paired immense incommensurables that defied history, as he did, by promoting the ideology of high culture at the same time he was involved in anticolonial political opposition. The unblended mix could only result in rescuing the "inventory" instead of the "infinity of traces" deposited by history.

By the same measure it also doesn't explain why he ignored Walter Benjamin and the deployment of a model of a politicized aesthetics against an aestheticized politics associated with fascism. In a sense the real model for Said was not the European theorists of high culture he so admired (whose own politics, especially in cold war afterlife, remained embarrassingly recessive at best) but the homegrown figure of Noam Chomsky, who offered a model in his recognition of the "instrumental connection between the Vietnam War and the notion of objective scholarship as it was applied to cover state-sponsored military research" (*O*, p. 11). However else we might feel about the particular choices Said made along his intellectual itinerary, what seems important now is the identity of the initial impulses of his project—akin to Sartre's "long work"—founded on the constant watchfulness of the oscillations of politics and culture as they inflected specific historical and contingent conditions comprising the conjunctural rustle he was living through.

The putative cultural turn that today more than ever dominates our humanistic disciplines was first recognized in the 1970s. Three books, published within eight years of each other, vocalized, in their own way, the conjuncture's embrace of culture: Hayden White's *Metahistory* (1973), Edward Said's *Orientalism* (1978), and Fredric Jameson's *Political Unconscious* (1981), prefigured years earlier in his groundbreaking book, *Marxism and Form* (1971). All three expressed the move to representation and the centrality of cultural-textual-production, whether it was in the act of constructing historical narratives or eliciting the unstated vocation of novelistic form. They thus recall for us a particular historical conjuncture that would willingly supply the demand for new ways to look at history, culture, and politics outside of explicit political arenas and generously offer new theoretical agendas capable of fulfilling this new mission. All, moreover, were produced in a charged moment marked by the ending of the Vietnam War—a truly globalized and globalizing event—mass political action (the peace and civil rights movements in the U.S.), and the unleashing of worldwide transformations inaugurated with Paris 1968 that literally altered the cultural and political landscape and were symptomized in the brief spectacle of "Third World"[3] triumphalism and the struggle against colonialism and its cold war factotum—modernization.[4] In this regard we must understand these texts as intimations of a revolution that never happened.[5] The resulting destabilization of American life, especially, was momentarily repaired by a resurgent neoliberal state devoted to firmly linking politics to the domain of the economy (the final identification of "democracy" and market capitalism), making it a subset of the commodity structure of society, which itself worked to produce a greater depoliticization of the population. Throughout the 1970s this pattern of an evolving, empowered state involved in promoting the greater integration of global capital prevailed in a number of advanced industrial societies like Japan, Great Britain, and Germany.

White's *Metahistory* set the tone for this turn to the status of representation by calling attention to the tropic strategies informing the construction of historical narratives. History lost its anchoring ground and the security of fixed referentiality because there now appeared to be no authority on which to privilege one account of meaning over another, no single and unassailable referent that would justify one narrative over another.[6] What this move signaled was the removal of any claim to grounding, other than language itself, and an ironic conception that announced that one historical account was as good as another. White's conception of history pre-

---

3. I am aware of the problematic nature of the category of Third World and the weakness of its conceptualization and the complaint registered by Aijaz Ahmad in his "Jameson's Rhetoric of Otherness and the 'National Allegory,'" *Social Text*, no. 17 (Fall 1987): 3–25; rpt. in *Marxist Literary Criticism*, ed. Terry Eagleton and Drew Milne (Oxford, 1996), pp. 375–98. But it is nonetheless true that this was the catchword used during the halcyon days of the sixties and beyond. But an earlier and, I believe, more incisive critique was made by Carl Pletsch, "The Three Worlds or the Division of Social Science Labor, Circa 1950–1975," *Comparative Studies in Society and History* 23, no. 4 (1981): 565–90.

4. See Kristin Ross, *May '68 and Its Afterlives* (Chicago, 2002).

5. See Albert Sohn-Rethel, *Intellectual and Manual Labour: A Critique of Epistemology* (Atlantic Highlands, N.J., 1978), p. xiii.

6. See Keith Jenkins, *Why History? Ethics and Postmodernity* (London, 1999), p. 3.

figured what Jameson would later count as postmodernity and its realization of the full achievement of modernity (the dream of all modernizers) and its dismissal of the claims of master narrative certainty and closure. Before Jameson threw himself into the domain of real subsumption, and its associated claim of a world fully embedded in the commodity relation, he proposed a way to read novelistic forms for their concealed and congealed ideological promptings, their political unconscious. Here, he clearly wished to emphasize the politics of representation itself, also derived from structural linguistics, over any attention to politics and the necessity to historicize such texts for what they were capable of saying about their moment from the depths of inner form. But Jameson, like White, was as much caught up in the world of endless representations he was advising others to historicize and, as a result, risked occupying a position exempt from the very historicizing regimes he was recommending. In later years this exemption won for him the charge that he was actually acclaiming the very postmodernity he so sensitively was analyzing as the cultural dominant of late capitalism. But it is true, nonetheless, that Jameson's discourse too often subordinated political economy to the aesthetic or cultural domains of representation or simply affirmed its status as a subset of the cultural dominant, as if culture possessed the capacity to completely metabolize politics. Jameson's cultural turn sandwiched the postmodern between aesthetics and economics and sacrificed to the terrain of representation precisely that "sense of culture as a battlefield" that divides claims into a field of contest, which, Perry Anderson once observed, in this context is "the plane of politics, understood as a space in its own right."[7] What links culture and politics, then, despite their often discrepant concerns, is the activity of critiquing representations—the necessity to evaluate artworks and discriminate the political conduct of state and society. In Jameson, and White to a certain extent, this separation seems to have disappeared.[8] What this fusion implies is the realization of a society that has reached the stage of real subsumption, so to speak, and the final effacement of the specter of unevenness associated with formal subsumption.

Said's *Orientalism*, the most Foucauldian of the trinity, was committed to revealing how representational strategies were implicated in figuring colonial otherness, from teasing out the political unconscious of novels to showing the involvement of scholarly research in constructing images of the colonized that would serve the interests of policy and domination. Here,

---

7. Perry Anderson, *The Origins of Postmodernity* (London, 1998), p. 134.

8. For an account of the necessarily discrepant relations between culture and politics, see Francis Mulhern, *Culture/Metaculture* (London, 2000), pp. 169-74.

culture and representation were plainly seen as functioning to satisfy the requirements of politics. Claiming a basis in authoritative knowledges and experience, these representations, undoubtedly mediated by received cultural conceits and political necessity, were indirectly linked to the colonizing project and supplied the means with which to deprive native populations of subjective agency while subjecting them to close surveillance and control. Said was interested in illuminating the political purposes of Orientalist representational strategies, and this meant demonstrating how imperialism always required culture to assist its political work, how, in fact, imaginative writing and scholarship combined into a discourse that was instrumentalized to serve the interests of national power.

Jameson and White went further than Said into a world dominated by culture and the endless circulation of representations; they emphasized the primacy of form and submerged a concern for the political or political economy deeper into the cultural hummus, implying that a distinct political terrain was indistinguishable from it. Said, however, was able to avoid the slide into the cultural turn by choosing another road. Both in his later writings and in his ceaseless defense of the Palestinian cause, he was forced to maintain a distance between his personal conception of high culture and everyday politics at the same time that he recognized how culture was invariably deployed to figure forms of political domination in the colonial historical experience. In this regard, what saved Said from being completely co-opted by the cultural turn was this contradiction between a devotion to high culture removed from his political activity in the cause of national independence and an intellectual view that saw culture constantly complicit in the promotion of imperialism. While his personal sense of culture remained apart from and above the everyday Palestinian political struggle, his principal writings never faltered in arguing how culture and politics were somehow inseparable yet distinct identities—what he described as an "unequal exchange"—implicated in the colonial and imperial project. But in Said it must also be recognized that the literary representatives of high culture were as easily enlisted as the academics by Orientalist discourse to "control, manipulate, even to incorporate, what is manifestly different" (*O*, p. 12). If, as he claimed, discourse is invariably shaped by the exchange with various kinds of power and that this recognition meant it was not simply representation but that it spoke to "'our' world," it would be important to ascertain what his own cultural preferences and style vocalized about his world.

We need, in any case, to examine more closely how Said, whose views on culture often bordered on the precious and dwelled in oxygen-thin elevations, timeless and eternal, a formalism that often disavowed "being in the world" he was advising others to accept, could at the same time entertain a totally separate and temporally bound everyday engagement dedicated to national independence against a colonizing power, how this remarkable conjoining of polar opposites between elitist European high culture and anticolonial struggle could be imagined in a world where, according to others, everything was culture and one representation therefore was as good as another. What Said's choice seemed to acknowledge was not the achievement of the final subsumption of labor to capital and the triumph of an imperializing value form but rather the messier and continuing presence of vast political and cultural unevenness and the persisting identity of semi-autonomous social forms that could still be politicized. We must, of course, recognize that promoting a modernist high culture and a nationalist cause share a fairly conservative and entirely bourgeois outlook and are, in some instances, historically connected—but not necessarily in Said's thinking. Yet notwithstanding the conceits of the high culture Said embraced, his commitment to resolving the Palestinian colonial question, as well as his critique of colonizing knowledge/power, put him in direct intellectual contact with the world outside of Euro-America and its putative postmodernity, a world more visibly manifesting the signs of unevenness and the identity of a politics not yet lost in the shadows of the cultural dominant.[9] In this respect, it should be remembered that Jameson, with the category of cultural revolution, nodded briefly in the direction of the Third World in *The Political Unconscious*. In this text, he presented the silhouette of an interpretive strategy filled with immense programmatic promise for understanding the historical passage of former colonies and Third World societies into the world of capitalist transformation that strangely was never fulfilled, even though it speaks more directly to the consequences of modernization than postcolonial discourse. Jameson was guided by a conception of the social formation worked out by Nicos Poulantzas (glossing Louis Althusser) that historical societies always display the "overlay and structural coexistence of *several* modes of production"; there is never the existence of a pure form, however dominant the mode, combining residues from earlier modes now assigned to dependent status to the new, all at the same time. Because these older survivals and vestiges remain partially unassimilated to the existing system, acting often as revenants from different pasts to remind contemporaries of what has been forgotten and possessing the capacity for sudden, unscheduled surfacing to haunt and disturb the present, they are always in a position to challenge the dominant mode of production and conceivably demand a space of their own, as Ernst Bloch observed in the rise of fascism

9. See Harry Harootunian, *History's Disquiet: Modernity, Cultural Practice, and the Question of Everyday Life* (New York, 2000).

in Germany in the 1930s. For Jameson, cultural revolution thus signaled the "moment in which the coexistence of various modes of production becomes visibly antagonistic," whereby the determinations from different domains combine to constitute a concentration of contradictions—an overdetermination—leading to the effect that Althusser once described as "ruptural unity" or the time of revolution. Poulantzas was convinced that one mode of production was distinguished from another by its choice of a particular form of articulation, which he called "matrix." Jameson designated these multiple matrices as the "object of study," which now occupied a new, encompassing, and "final horizon" that he named as cultural revolution.[10] This coalescence of coexisting residues from different but synchronic modes of production marked the instant of transformation when the past in the present opened up to the future to faintly resemble a reenactment of Heiddeggerian ecstatic temporality, which seems to have shadowed the experience of all societies as they passed into the world of capitalist modernity. Here Jameson recalled the "incomplete experiment" of China's recent cultural revolution that actually had drawn upon an earlier episode (May 1919) in a massive effort to inaugurate modernization. But far from presenting a static, synchronic countenance, mobilizing the historic figure of the Chinese cultural revolution symbolized a repetition in the present of a prior example of politicizing culture to move China temporally beyond its moribund, semicolonial warlordism. Later, Jameson envisioned Third World literary production as an expansion of national allegory, as if, in fact, cultural embourgeoisement was a necessary condition of the diverse national independence movements.[11] White's *Metahistory*, however, was as culturally hermetic as the literary histories of Auerbach or Curtius, Said's favorite critics. White's narrative rarely if ever strayed from the European compound, and his tropological account managed to affirm the very cultural endowment and nation form that mediated the colonization of the rest of the world. This was startling because the background noise to *Metahistory*'s composition was the Vietnam War. Said's *Orientalism*, in contrast, aimed (albeit indirectly) to undermine both the very historical knowledge White was rescuing for art and the narrative forms his analysis had put up for canonization. By demonstrating how knowledge had been used to repress the experience of the excluded second term, the outside to Euro-America's inside, Said's tactic sought to move beyond the heritage of the European past and avoid the trap of falling into assimilating cultural

10. Fredric Jameson, *The Political Unconscious: Narrative as a Socially Symbolic Act* (Ithaca, N.Y., 1981), p. 95.

11. See Ahmad, "Jameson's Rhetoric of Otherness and the 'National Allegory.'"

production to Western exemplars. We should, in this connection, recall the attack launched by Aijaz Ahmad, who insisted on associating Said's project with the migration of scholars and intellectuals from Asia and Africa to the metropolitan West that, in his assessment, provided them a comfortable but distant perspective from which to envisage and construct a program around colonialism, postcoloniality, identity, diaspora, and so on. Despite the accusation of apparent descent, Said forcefully opened up, whether intentionally or not, the long-suppressed spectacle of unevenness between culture and politics that was explicitly being played out in the world beyond Euro-America—the site of its imperial conquest and colonial expropriation since the nineteenth century. More importantly, the opening to the colonial world and its endless capacity for the reproduction of unevenness dramatized the performance of a leading principle everywhere capitalist accumulation had established its regime, one whose defining lineaments had not yet been disguised by postmodern pastiche. In this sense, Said's project reminds us of a path that was still accessible in the 1970s, a survivor of conjunctural traces, a path always on the verge of being shut down, as we have seen with depressing regularity in the academy today and among so-called public intellectuals of our time.

The task of identifying a temporalizing politics rooted in concrete anticolonial struggle was built into Said's vision of colonial discourse, in spite of being situated in the metropolitan West. But it was often delayed and even diverted on occasion by its subsequent postcolonial inflections, which in the name of radicalizing his critique, eventually turned to address issues concerning the relationship between colonizer and colonized and settled on the search for some sort of prescient subjective agency rooted in claims of cultural authenticity rather than contemporary political struggle in the postcolony that may very well have been already prefigured during the colonial episode. In this sense, postcolonial discourse managed to conform more closely to culture's omnivorous appetite than to Said's initial colonial critique. Yet, postcolonialism, owing to Said's own slippage, was in a position to recuperate the conception of a unified West, much like Western Marxism, as a stand-in for the polar opposite of the Orient. In its practice, postcolonialism conduced to produce the effect of "dematerializing" as a condition that would pave the way to making the "Orient" the fixed space of an "alternative modernity."[12] While it would be wrong to accuse Said of having given us the category of an "alternative modernity," it is, nonetheless, important to recall that his appeal to the West as the enunciator of Orien-

---

12. See Neil Lazarus, "The Fetish of the 'West' in Postcolonial Theory," in *Marxism, Modernity, and Postcolonial Studies,* ed. Crystal Bartolovich and Lazarus (Cambridge, 2002), p. 55.

talist discourse never referred to the capitalist mode of production as such, thus clearing the path for the category's appearance, even though he insisted upon the "material effectiveness of Orientalism" (*O*, p. 23).[13] In this gesture we can see both the specter of Auerbach's valorization of a culturally unified West and Said's reluctance to abandon its categorical force. But, with the postcolonial dedication to an "alternative modernity," we have already entered the precinct of the cultural dominant—the colonizing space of culture—which demands a parallel move from considerations of time and its relationship to space to spatial primacy and the "end of temporality," whereby even the conjuncture loses its momentary and historical status to become a fixed and unmoving countenance. What the figure of alternative modernity, and its numerous offshoots, supplies is simply a supplement to the lack the concept of a unified West invariably demands of its other, postcolonial discourse's own version of a cultural mode of production that seeks only to be included among the counted. If, in any case, we are to radicalize Said's program, materialize it, which is what any further conversation about his work should be about, we must look elsewhere than to an all-incorporating culturalism.

It seems to me that such discussion should begin with Said's recognition of the discrepant realms of culture and politics and with his refusal to dissolve the latter into the former. We know that he barely escaped—by an unknowing espousal of a fetishized, unified West—the expansive culturalism that both Western Marxism and postcolonial discourse embraced in order to make it into a vocation. But his deep, passionate, and enduring involvement in the everyday political struggle against a colonial power still offers invitation to rewind and rethink precisely the way we (perhaps "laborpower" is more accurate), individually and collectively, must manage to resist and even "*elude*" our assigned status as effect of pure commodity or value form imposed by capital's logic.[14]

Hence, we must see in his embracing of high culture and engagement of the daily struggle of Palestinian independence the sign of an unevenness he actually lived, between a politics that was always about time and temporality and a culture that remained locked in fixed space if not in fantasy. At the same time, he recognized, like Gramsci, the discrepant valences governing the relationship between culture and politics, accounting for its fearful asymmetry; he was responsive to how this difference always inflected the historically specific, the contingent.[15] Colonial and postcolonial studies

13. On the conceptual emptiness of the category of alternative modernity, see Harootunian, "Quartering the Millennium," *Radical Philosophy*, no. 116 (Nov.–Dec. 2002): 21–29.

14. Étienne Balibar, *The Philosophy of Marx*, trans. Chris Turner (London, 1985), p. 101.

15. See Mulhern, *Culture/Metaculture*, p. 171.

originated in textualization to make English departments the virtual out-posts of colonial memory. But the politics of Palestinian anticolonial strug-gle still exceeded this static textualization of culture and is still writing its very different history out of the immediate experience of an everydayness in the now. By contrast, postcolonial discourse on knowledge/power and identity, once it moved away from the actual afterlives of decolonization, simply passed into the past and memory, substituting forms of difference for genuine political, social, economic, and cultural unevenness and their respective demands for resolute action. In this connection a second register of unevenness is hinted at in Said's cultivation of the terrain of colonial power and domination. While he backed off from actually addressing the instance of unevenness introduced by capitalist colonial powers, content only to contemplate the unequal exchange of textual forms figuring the Ori-ent implicated in "dominating and having authority over it," Said, still, per-haps inadvertently, disclosed the spectacle of what clearly was before him but that escaped his vision—colonialism as a vast domain of unsynchron-ized synchrony stemming from the reproduction of capital accumulation. What seems important about this opening toward colonialism is the spec-ularity of the unevenness, both constituting its sign and defining its rela-tionship to the industrial states of Euro-America, and its capacity to escape its imprisonment in a different temporality to become the mirror of our nature. Specifically, it was precisely this experience among late, so-called developers—colonies—that actually made available to the "enfeebled cen-ters" both the recognition of the temporal immanence of unevenness and its existence in our own backyard.[16] Said never went as far as either Samir Amin and Cabral, not to forget Takeuchi, who all saw history, as well as culture, as the site of a persisting unevenness that could only be grasped in the historical specificity of political struggle, not in the act of awarding sub-jectivity to the marginalized whose agency derived from an irreducible and fixed ground of cultural authenticity. But we also know, as his later work in the *London Review of Books* amply demonstrates, that he was able to ac-knowledge the existence of immense material unevenness reflecting the pat-tern of landholding settlements in the Palestinian everyday, which, like the ghost in the machine, was always at the heart of the conflict with Israel. That it was there in the colonies is still a reminder that it is here and everywhere as part of an "infinity of traces" to which we have yet to attend.

16. In *The Geopolitical Aesthetic: Cinema and Space in the World System* (Bloomington, Ind., 1992), p. 155, Jameson refers to the "developing Third World" and the disappearance of what used to be called the local in a world divided into center and periphery. In late capitalism, the postmodern aesthetic no longer obeys this division of labor and "expressions of the marginally uneven and the unevenly developed issuing from a recent experience of capitalism are often more intense and powerful, more . . . deeply . . . meaningful than anything the enfeebled center still finds itself able to say."

Said, Palestine, and the Humanism of Liberation

Saree Makdisi

"The fact of the matter," wrote Edward Said in 1979, "is that today Palestine does not exist, except as a memory, or, more importantly, as an idea, a political and human experience, and an act of sustained popular will." What I want to propose in this essay is that this complex vision of Palestine not merely as a place but as an idea, an experience, and a will—inexorably tied to a living people—not only animated Said's work on behalf of the Palestinians. It also provided the conceptual and political foundation for his understanding of humanism as well as for his enormous contributions to critical theory and the field of colonial studies, a field that was inaugurated by his work on Orientalism.

In distinguishing Palestine as an idea from Palestine as experience and will, however, Said recognized that the struggle for the *idea* of Palestine, though tied to its people and their cause, is somehow larger than Palestine itself, that it is a struggle animated by a sense of justice and a concept of humanism not predicated on claims of ethnic, racial, or religious exclusivity but, rather, on inclusivity and community. Precisely because it was born of the most brutal—almost literally inhuman—conditions, what Said identified as the idea of Palestine is a struggle for the articulation of a new sense of what it means to be human.

Indeed, the struggle for what Said called the idea of Palestine takes on its particular significance precisely because of the nature of what it set out to oppose, namely, Zionism. In this context it must be remembered that, given its emergence at the height not only of European interest in ethnically based nationalism but also of the age of European empire, it was inevitable that mainstream "political" Zionism (as opposed to the "cultural" Zionism of, say, Judah Magnes) would articulate its vision according to epistemological terms provided by or borrowed from a racially and ethnically fueled imperialism—principally, the epistemological framework opposing a European self to a non-European other. As a range of writers from Hannah Arendt to Amil Alkalai to Said himself consistently warned, the opposition between this Zionist self and the Palestinian other was essential to political Zionism from its very beginning; and it has remained institutionalized in the practices and policies of the Israeli state to this day. It should hardly have been a surprise, then, that when the Zionist fantasy of discovering a land without a people for a people without a land collided with the actual (albeit somewhat awkward and inconvenient) reality of a land *with* a people—the Palestinians—the earliest Zionist spokesmen were uncompromising. "The penniless native population," wrote Theodor Herzl, the father of political Zionism, would simply have to be "spirited away" to make room for Jewish immigrants from Europe.

Writing a little further into the execution of the Zionist project in Palestine, Vladimir Jabotinsky, the founder of revisionist Zionism, was, according to his sympathetic biographer, "realistic" and "stern" in making preparations for what he frankly acknowledged to be the colonial takeover of Palestine by alien Europeans. "Every indigenous people will resist alien settlers as long as they see any hope of ridding themselves of the danger of foreign settlement," Jabotinsky pointed out. "As long as the Arabs [that is, the Palestinians] preserve a gleam of hope that they will succeed in getting rid of us, nothing in the world can cause them to relinquish this hope, precisely because they are not a rabble but a living people. And a living people will be ready to yield on such fateful issues only when they have given up all hope of getting rid of the alien settlers." Thus, he concluded that settlement could develop only "under the protection of a force that is not dependent on the local population, behind an iron wall which they will be powerless to break down."[1] David Ben-Gurion himself recognized that "there is no example in history of a people saying we agree to renounce our country, let another people come and settle here and outnumber us."[2] On

1. Quoted in Avi Shlaim, *The Iron Wall: Israel and the Arab World* (New York, 2001), pp. 13, 14, 13.

2. Quoted in Edward W. Said, "Truth and Reconciliation," *Al-Ahram Weekly*, 14–20 Jan. 1999, weekly.ahram.org.eg/1999/412/op2.htm; if he were a Palestinian leader, Ben-Gurion mused, he would never make peace with Israel. "That is natural," he pointed out; "we have taken their

SAREE MAKDISI is professor of English at the University of California, Los Angeles. He is the author of *William Blake and the Impossible History of the 1790s* (2003) and *Romantic Imperialism: Universal Empire and the Culture of Modernity* (1998).

the very eve of the catastrophe of 1948, Joseph Weitz, the administrator responsible for overseeing Jewish immigration into Palestine—and the founder of the Jewish National Fund—argued that "it must be clear that there is no room for both peoples together in this country . . . . The only solution is a Palestine without Arabs . . . . And there is no other way than to transfer the Arabs from here to the neighboring countries, to transfer all of them; not one village, not one tribe should be left."

"Palestine was not divided," as the Israeli historian Ilan Pappé points out; "it was destroyed, and most of its people expelled."[3] And, in fact, the vision of Jabotinsky, Herzl, and Weitz was accomplished precisely through the destruction of Palestine and—under Ben-Gurion's command—the forcible expulsion of most of its native population in 1948. Though it was initially denied in a pall of mythmaking (which still shrouds American Zionism), the Palestinian account of what happened in 1948 has, since the 1980s, been thoroughly documented and verified by a number of Israeli historians, including Pappé, Benny Morris, Avi Shlaim, Simha Flapan, and others—not always, it should be added, with particular sympathy for the Palestinian experience. Morris, for example, has been particularly forthcoming in his frank account of 1948. "There are circumstances that justify ethnic cleansing," he argues in a recent interview in *Ha'aretz*. Just as "the great American democracy could not have been created without the annihilation of the Indians," he adds, in 1948, "a Jewish state would not have come into being without the uprooting of 700,000 Palestinians. Therefore it was necessary to uproot them. There was no choice but to expel that population. It was necessary to cleanse the hinterland and cleanse the border areas and cleanse the main roads. It was necessary to cleanse the villages from which our convoys and our settlements were being fired on." The only problem Morris sees with what happened in 1948 is that Ben-Gurion did not go far enough: "Even though he understood the demographic issue and the need to establish a Jewish state without a large Arab minority, he got cold feet during the war. In the end, he faltered." Perhaps, Morris muses, "if he was already engaged in expulsion, maybe he should have done a complete job." For "if the end of the story turns out to be a gloomy one for the Jews, it will be because Ben-Gurion did not complete the transfer in 1948. Because he left a large

---

country. Sure, God promised it to us, but what does that matter to them? Our God is not theirs. We come from Israel, it's true, but two thousand years ago, and what is that to them? There has been antisemitism, the Nazis, Hitler, Auschwitz, but was that their fault? They only see one thing: we have come here and stolen their country. Why should they accept that?" (quoted in Nahum Goldmann, *The Jewish Paradox*, trans. Steve Cox [New York, 1978], p. 99).

3. Ilan Pappé, "The Geneva Bubble," *London Review of Books*, 8 Jan. 2004, www.lrb.co.uk/v26/n01/papp01_.html; hereafter abbreviated "GB."

and volatile demographic reserve in the West Bank and Gaza and within Israel itself."[4]

Even if it was not a "complete job," the Zionist ethnic cleansing of Palestine in 1948 was remarkably effective. Moshe Dayan remarked in 1969, "We came to this country which was already populated by Arabs, and we are establishing a Hebrew, that is a Jewish, state here. In considerable areas of the country [6 percent, to be precise] we bought the land from the Arabs. Jewish villages were built in the place of Arab villages. You do not even know the name of these Arab villages, and I do not blame you, because these geography books no longer exist; not only do the books not exist, the Arab villages are not there either . . . . There is not one place in this country that did not have a former Arab population." Like Morris, Dayan was admirable in his frankness; over four hundred Palestinian villages were, in fact, systematically pulverized in 1947–48.

Thus it should be obvious (but, remarkably, it is not) that a concept of ethnic or demographic separation—a biopolitics of the crudest and most reductive form—has been central to the logic of political Zionism as it has been imagined and practiced from its inception up to the present day: not just in *militant* Zionism but in *peaceful* Zionism, not just in the Zionism of the settlements but in the Zionism underlying the absurd set of "negotiations" that got underway in Oslo in 1993 and, ever since Oslo, in all those plans for demographic separation that go under the banner of "peace initiatives."[5] Although with the breakdown of this so-called peace process it has become commonplace in liberal circles in the United States and Europe to bemoan the ascendancy of Ariel Sharon (and to mourn nostalgically for the supposedly more pacific days and ideals of Yitzhak Rabin and, hence, a desperate return to the peace process), it is historically naive and politically disingenuous to imagine that what Sharon stands for marks some kind of aberration in the history of Zionism. There is not a thing that Sharon does (or would like to do) to the Palestinians that was not imagined, enabled, or actually set in motion in one way or another by the history of Zionism and by previous Israeli governments—above all, that of Rabin, whose obsessive calculus of domination and occupation was given full expression in the Oslo process. There can be no equivocation on this point: what drives Israeli policy toward the Palestinians, in an uninterrupted narrative that runs from 1897 to 1948 to 1967 through the peace process of the 1990s and up to the apartheid wall and the so-called Sharon plan of 2004, is Zionism's inex-

4. Benny Morris, "On Ethnic Cleansing," interview by Ari Shavit, *New Left Review* 26 (Mar.– Apr. 2004): 42, 43, 42, 44.

5. See Azmi Beshara, "A Short History of Apartheid," *Al Ahram Weekly*, 8–14 Jan. 2004, weekly.ahram.org.eg/2004/672/op10.htm

haustible will to separate Jews from non-Jews, to separate and, as Meron
Benvenisti (Israel's former deputy mayor of Jerusalem) puts it, to dominate
and oppress precisely through the logic, the discourse, and the biopolitical
practice of *separation.*[6]

In any case, what was on offer at Oslo was a territorially discontinuous
Palestinian Bantustan (divided into over sixty disconnected fragments) that
would have had no control over water resources, borders, or airspace, much
less an independent economy, currency, or financial system, and whose sovereignty, nominal as it was, would be punctuated by heavily fortified Israeli
colonies and an autonomous Jewish road network, all of which would be
effectively under Israeli army control. Even this, however, was never realized. When the whole process finally broke down irreparably after Ehud
Barak's supposedly magnanimous Camp David offer in 2000 (which, insofar as any such offer can be said to have been made, was essentially more
of the same that had already been on offer since Oslo, "leaving about 15
percent of original Palestine for the Palestinians, in the form of discrete
cantons bisected by highways, settlements, army camps and walls"
["GB"]),[7] the Israelis had redeployed from exactly 40 percent of the Gaza
Strip, less than 18 percent of the West Bank, and not a square inch of Jerusalem.

On the contrary, all through the period of negotiations the Israelis continued and even accelerated the pace of building and expanding their colonies in the West Bank and Gaza as well as in East Jerusalem: the crudest
form of biopolitics. When the negotiations got under way at Oslo in 1993,
there were some one hundred thousand settlers in the Israeli colonies; all
through the period of negotiations this number increased, finally doubling
by 2000. There are now some two hundred thousand Israeli colonists in the
West Bank and another seven thousand or so in Gaza. In addition, a further

6. See Meron Benvenisti, "Founding a Binational State," *Ha'aretz,* 22 Apr. 2004, www.fmep.org/
analysis/benvenisti_Haaretz_FoundingABinationalstate.html; hereafter abbreviated "FBS."

7. Ehud Barak allegedly promised to the Palestinians during the Camp David negotiations in
2000 the "return" of over 90 percent of the West Bank, a Palestinian "capital" in East Jerusalem
(actually, the suburb of Abu Dis), and so on. As we now know from the accounts of American and
Israeli negotiators (but not, sadly, the Palestinians), Barak actually made no offer as such at Camp
David, since nothing was in writing and whatever was said was communicated verbally via
President Clinton. But insofar as Barak can be said to have made an offer, what he was offering,
based on a formula proposed in May 2000, was more or less what had already been on the table at
Oslo in 1995—with the added caveat that the Palestinians would have to formally surrender their
right of return as well as unconditionally declare the conflict permanently over, that is, subject to
no further negotiations. This, ultimately, even Arafat was unable to do—so the negotiations broke
down. And the new intifada erupted in the fall of 2000: a popular revolt both against the
corruption and stupidity of the Palestinian leadership and against the ongoing and the ever more
draconian Israeli military occupation. For more on Camp David and the peace process in general,
see Tanya Reinhart, *Israel/Palestine: How to End the War of 1948* (New York, 2002).

two hundred thousand Israelis occupy land, houses, and new colonies in Arab East Jerusalem as well as in the vastly expanded metropolitan Jewish Jerusalem, which the Israelis created as a wedge deliberately driven into the West Bank. Jewish Jerusalem by itself eats up a significant portion of the whole territory—though by a rhetorical sleight of hand it does not count (for the Israelis) as "occupied territory" and hence was not counted as part of the West Bank in the various Israeli "offers" at Oslo or Camp David.

Even more significantly, however, the redeployments, such as they were, disguised the extraordinary intensification of the occupation that the Oslo process had enabled. Whereas before Oslo the West Bank and Gaza had been more or less territorially coherent internally (however cut off from the outside world and subject to the routine closures, curfews, and lockdowns associated with the military occupation), the Oslo negotiations led to the generation of dozens of separate Palestinian enclaves, many of them less than two square kilometers in size. Each of these was isolated from all the others by a series of Israeli checkpoints and roadblocks, and to get past these Israeli roadblocks required authorizations and permits, which the occupation forces made it extraordinarily difficult to obtain. The result was the nearly total paralysis of Palestinian life on the West Bank and in Gaza. For example, a journey from Hebron to Ramallah, which should take about an hour even with traffic, could now take up to ten hours when it was possible at all—that is, when the Israelis opened the checkpoints and allowed Palestinians with "proper" permits through. Rarely, if ever, would Palestinians from the West Bank be allowed into Jerusalem, the very center of Palestinian life, much less into Israel itself. On various occasions, the entire Palestinian population—over three million people—would be summarily confined to their homes in order to "safeguard" Jewish holidays or various Zionist commemorations. As I write, in fact, the whole Palestinian population of the West Bank and Gaza is under collective house arrest—a shoot-on-sight curfew—so that Israelis can joyously celebrate the founding of their state. It should go without saying that such confinements, and the other routine measures of collective punishment with which Israel abuses the Palestinians living under its military occupation, are flagrant violations of international law (the Fourth Geneva Convention, for one).

Zionism's zeal for ethnic separation and exclusion is what is evident in all this. As institutionalized by the so-called peace process, the machine of Israeli military occupation seeks to break its victims not simply by shooting and killing them but by grinding them down with mundane details—with permits, rules, quotas, rations, curfews, and so on—for this is an occupation that turns everyday existence into (at best) little more than a nightmare of mundane details. This is why a merely theoretical account of the struggle between Israelis and Palestinians will never be able to come to terms with its essentially banal quotidian reality. For in the West Bank and Gaza, human life has been reduced to its naked rudiments. The ever-expanding network of Jewish colonies, bypass roads, and closed areas, and the corresponding matrix of barriers, checkpoints, chokepoints, curfews, and rarely granted permits for non-Jews (that is to say, Palestinians) that the Oslo process greatly accelerated and intensified have resulted in a situation on the ground in the occupied territories in which even the most fundamental and mundane aspects of human necessity (birth, death, housing, eating, working, farming, access to water, movement, health care, education—that is, the matters of who one is, where one can go, what one can do) are comprehensively determined by the ontological categories and narratives of European racism as they have been embodied, expressed, and institutionalized in Zionism—in other words, in the biopolitical policies of the State of Israel and the military occupation that it has chosen to continue to impose for almost four decades with no end in sight.

And, in terms of separation, what goes for the Occupied Territories goes, more or less, for Israel proper. Israel is a country that was founded, and that rests today, on an ineradicable distinction—nothing less than an explicit, socially engineered apartheid—between Jews and non-Jews. Israel, as Tony Judt put it recently, is "an anachronism." "It is an oddity among modern nations not—as its more paranoid supporters assert—because it is a *Jewish* state and no one wants the Jews to have a state," Judt argues, "but because it is a Jewish *state* in which one community—Jews—is set above others, in an age when that sort of state has no place."[8] Almost all the land of Israel proper (that is, 93 percent of Israel within its pre-1967 boundaries) is officially held "in perpetuity by the Jewish people" and cannot legally be rented, much less sold, to non-Jews (including the land's original owners). In a state in which life is saturated with the discourses of racial, ethnic, and religious distinctions, Israel's Palestinian population (which today constitutes fully 20 percent of the total but is legally restricted to 2 percent of the land) faces enormous institutionalized harassment and discrimination in matters not merely of land use and ownership but also of employment, marriage, education, and social security—all the stuff of what might be normal life. While even some of the most open-minded Israelis erupt in fury at any mention of the right of return of Palestinians who were born in Haifa, in Nazareth, in Jerusalem and then evicted from their homes at gunpoint by heavily armed European immigrants in 1948, anyone Jewish from anywhere in the world has the right (according to the Israelis) to claim instant citizenship

---

8. Tony Judt, "Israel: The Alternative," *New York Review of Books*, 23 Oct. 2003, pp. 8, 10.

in Israel. And while they watch Jewish people from Latvia, Estonia, and Ethiopia—whose attachment to "the land of Israel" rests only on the most spurious biblical claims—arrive and immediately assume the full mantle of citizens' rights, the Palestinians of Israel are reminded every day, in the land of their birth and ancestry, of their status as barely tolerated second- and third-class citizens. Meanwhile, all around them, there swirls ever more feverishly the discussion in Hebrew of the final solutions to the Palestinian "problem": expulsion, transfer, eradication in one form or another—"politicide," as the Israeli writer Baruch Kimerling puts it.

This is not the place, however, to do anything more than remind readers of the kind and the extent of discrimination faced by non-Jews in a state that frequently indulges in debates over "who is a Jew"[9] and in territories militarily occupied by that state. The Israeli government has literalized and actualized all the logics, apparatuses, discourses, and practices associated with the worst, the ugliest, the most violent and draconian forms of European racism, for decades on end, without the slightest regard for the by-now pitiful, almost dying, appeals of the people whose lives it has smashed, whose history it has annihilated, and whose future it has all but destroyed.

My point here is not simply to recount what Israel and Zionism have done to the Palestinians but, rather, to recall that from the earliest days of the Zionist project, in Israel and the Occupied Territories alike, the role allotted to the Palestinians in the narrative of Zionism has been, at best, that of inconvenience, obstacle, impediment, and, in sum, that of other to a ruthlessly violent ethnotheological discourse of alterity in which there has only ever been room for one self. As Said himself argued in these pages, it is precisely in this sense that Zionism, with its "ideology of difference," recapitulates the binary structure basic to all modern imperialism, predicated necessarily on opposition between a fully human self and a not-quite-human other. And if the problem for all the great anti-imperial struggles of the twentieth century was the question of how to articulate a logic of the human—and, hence, a form of humanism—that does not merely recapitulate or, worse, invert the rightfully discredited logic of imperialism and *its* own brand of humanism, this problem has a particular urgency in the context of Palestine. For, lurking in the wings, there have always been those Palestinian responses to Zionism that call for an absolutism and hence a violence commensurate with the baleful absolutism of Zionism itself.

For Said, the idea of Palestine was always something that transcended

---

9. See, for example, Elli Wohlgelernter, "'Who's a Jew' Battle Flares in Jerusalem," *Forward*, 4 July 2003.

the sort of mindless reactive violence expressed by those Palestinians—ever a minority—who see no other choice than to play the role of Caliban to Israel's Prospero. Thus the idea of Palestine was always, in Said's work, inseparable from the larger humanist project on which he had embarked, a humanist project that sought to rescue humanism itself from the larger claims of European imperialism with which it had come into the world. We must bear in mind here that in elaborating his form of humanism, Said had absorbed the lesson offered by Frantz Fanon, whose great hope was for the Third World to articulate a vision of the human that did not merely send back to Europe a nauseating reflection of itself but, instead, involved embarking on what he called a "new history of man." "When I search for Man in the technique and the style of Europe," Fanon wrote, "that same Europe where they [are] never done talking of Man, and where they never [stop] proclaiming they [are] only anxious for the welfare of Man, [though] today we know with what sufferings humanity has paid for every one of their triumphs of the mind . . . , I see only a succession of negations of man, and an avalanche of murders." In calling for the Third World to set afoot what he called "a new man," however, Fanon did not intend the negation of Europe, much less its destruction. On the contrary, he envisioned its salvation and redemption in a new concept of humanity premised on the dialectical synthesis of those opposing forces into an altogether new form of life, something quite distinct from either the old colonial logic of binary distinctions—separating, as thesis from antithesis, white from black, north from south, west from east, and human from inhuman—or the phantasmatic search for a hybrid in-betweenness that might imagine itself to have slipped unsullied and uncompromised through the rigid ontological barriers of colonial power.

Said's humanism drew on and spoke to the great oppositional legacy of Fanon, Nietzsche, and Blake as much as the more narrowly conceived humanism of Arnold and Eliot, with whom he has been sometimes reductively associated because of his stubborn refusal to abandon a discourse of the human even in the face of poststructuralist critique. "By humanism," Said wrote, "I mean first of all attempting to dissolve Blake's mind-forg'd manacles so as to be able to use one's mind historically and rationally for the purposes of reflective understanding. Moreover humanism is sustained by a sense of community with other interpreters and other societies and periods: strictly speaking therefore there is no such thing as an isolated humanist." Humanism, Said added, is also "the only and I would go as far as saying the final resistance we have against the inhuman practices and injustices that have disfigured human history." For Said, then, humanism involved developing a logic of being-in-common, in which the task of interpretation was never to be confined to books, music, and art but also applied to life and to humanity itself. He conceived humanity as a collective, absorptive, embracing, heterogeneous, and infinitely open-ended *striving* rather than the violent, fractured, binary conception of humanity underlying European imperialism, with its opposition of the human to the non-human or subhuman and of self to other—the conception, in short, on which Zionism stands. Indeed, in the context of the question of Palestine, from which in Said's case this kind of humanism emerged, humanism itself can ultimately be understood only as a response to the logic of Zionism, even if it is also more than that as well. In other words, the idea of Palestine for which Said worked amounted to both an engagement with *and* a transcendence of the distorting, violent, and, finally, quite inhuman logic of Zionism.

For Said, however, this counterlogic of humanism was never simply an exercise in idealist thought; rather, it is something that actually lives in the Palestinian people. It manifests, for example, in the fact that to this day the Palestinian people as a whole want and stand for something more than merely a reflexively violent reaction to Zionism. They have not stopped talking of alternative futures, of cooperation, of working together with Israel's Jews toward a happier and shared future, and hence of building on an understanding of what it means to develop a human community *with* rather than *against* other human beings. This talking continues despite all the suffering inflicted on them for decades by an implacable enemy sworn to destroy every trace of their collective existence.

No one expressed the idea of Palestine more eloquently than Said himself. "Palestinians present themselves as interlocutors with the Israelis for peace," he wrote after the historic meeting in Algiers in 1988 in which the Palestine National Council, the Palestinian parliament-in-exile of which Said was then a member, offered to recognize Israel and work toward a peaceful negotiation of the conflict (an offer that was to be secretly co-opted and subverted by the negotiations entered into at Oslo). He continued,

> We say to the Israelis, . . . live with us, but not on top of us. Your logic, by which you forecast an endless siege, is doomed, the way all colonial adventures are doomed. We know that Israelis possess a heritage of suffering, and that the Holocaust looms large over their present thought. But we Palestinians cannot be expected merely to submit to military rule and the denial of our human and political rights . . . . Therefore we must together formulate the modes of existence, of mutuality and sharing, those modes that can take us beyond fear and suffering into the future, and an extraordinarily interesting and impressive future at that.

Thus, for Said, the idea of Palestine, and the larger humanism of liberation that it represented for him, is affirmative and productive. Not an idealized abstraction to which reality should have to adjust itself, humanism for Said is, as Marx put it, a "*real* movement which abolishes the present state of things"[10] and which is creative of new relationships, expressive of the desire for the immanent generation of new identities, new forms of knowledge, new forms of thought, new communities of expression and of being—while never forgetting or ignoring the history of suffering from which the idea of Palestine emerged. Spinozan in quality if not in name, the ultimate horizon of the heterogeneous and infinitely open-ended striving that Said called humanism is the production of new forms of life, life understood in the Spinozan—or, for that matter, the Blakean—sense as indeterminate, expansive, and existing precisely in the connections and affects that tie human beings together.

If Said's sense of humanism was in effect about a dissolution of the barriers between public and private—hence, his tireless calls for intellectuals to be more engaged with public concerns and less introspectively self-obsessed, withdrawn from the public realm, and confined to the restrictive boundaries of their disciplinary commitments—that is because what most interested him was our capacity as human beings for determining and creating new publics, new communities, new forms of life. This was the basis of the critical and theoretical project that Said launched in *Orientalism* and, indeed, even before *Orientalism* in *Beginnings,* which is a study of the concept of potential. Much of his work was committed to elaborating such forms of potential across various disciplines and media (from art and music to politics and, of course, literature) and to contesting and reading against the grain those forms of art and politics that, on the contrary, sought to elaborate or to ally themselves with a logic of domination, occupation, and power.

This brings us inevitably to the question of what, in the context of Palestine, a politics of genuine humanism and liberation might look like, or, to be more precise, what such a politics *did* look like, according to Said himself. In order to address that point and, hence, to anticipate the future—and maybe even the possible peaceful resolution—of the struggle between Zionism and the Palestinians with any degree of realism, it is essential to take stock, even briefly, of how the situation has stood since the irreparable breakdown of the Oslo process in 2000.

10. See Karl Marx, *The German Ideology,* in *The Marx-Engels Reader,* ed. Robert C. Tucker, 2d ed. (New York, 1978), p. 162.

The results of the second intifada, whose eruption marked the decisive end of Oslo, have been devastating for the Palestinians (not to mention the hundreds of Israeli civilians killed or wounded by Palestinian counterviolence). Around thirty-five hundred Palestinians have been killed, and a further thirty-five thousand wounded, many seriously, thanks to the Israeli policy of shooting to inflict massive injury—blindness, amputation, paralysis—rather than outright death. The overwhelming majority of Palestinian casualties (85 percent) have been unarmed civilians, a disproportionate number of them children. The Israeli army has been charged by numerous international human rights and medical organizations, including the normally quite reticent International Red Cross, of a wildly excessive use of force in confronting Palestinian demonstrators, most of them, as I've said, unarmed. In a series of extrajudicial executions, the Israelis have also used laser-guided antitank missiles, high-explosive tank projectiles, and even one-ton aerial bombs to assassinate individual human "targets," along with anyone else who happens to be in the way. Ambulances and rescue crews are routinely prevented from saving the injured. During the ferocious Israeli onslaught against the refugee camp in Jenin in April 2002, for example, medical services workers were denied access to the camp for almost two weeks. Ambulances had to wait at the surrounding Israeli checkpoints while countless wounded Palestinians—civilians and guerrillas alike—bled to death or died of injuries that might otherwise have been treatable.[11]

Since June 2002, when Israel reoccupied the West Bank, over a million Palestinians have been kept under a system of intensified curfews and closures that, at any given time, confines tens of thousands or even hundreds of thousands of men, women, and children—and sometimes the entire Palestinian population—to their homes for days or weeks on end. There were, for example, almost 6,000 hours of curfew for the Palestinians of Hebron in 2003 (which is the equivalent of 241 days, more than half a year of continuous curfew). The city's 415 heavily armed Jewish colonists—who seriously believe themselves to be on a sacred mission from God—are, of course, free to roam at will and to inflict such harassment on the native population (130,000 Palestinians) as they see fit.

Unimaginably, the situation in Gaza is even worse. As though it weren't bad enough that the 1.5 million Palestinians of Gaza are crammed into the territory's most barren land (giving it the dubious distinction of being the most densely populated area on earth), the 7,000 Israeli settlers there are

---

11. The Human Rights Watch investigation into the attack on Jenin concluded that "Israeli forces committed serious violations of international humanitarian law, some amounting *prima facie* to war crimes" (Peter Bouckaert, Miranda Sissons, and Johanna Bjorken, "Jenin: IDF Military Operations," http://www.hrw.org/reports/2002/israel3/israel0502–01.htm#P49_1774).

spread out into colonies whose location deliberately disrupts the territorial contiguity of the 60 percent or so of Gaza that the Palestinians nominally control, dividing it into chunks linked together by Israeli army checkpoints that open and close at random intervals and can shut down altogether at whim for days. Hermetically sealed off from the outside world by a network of electric fences and ditches—its labor force now entirely irrelevant and extraneous to the Israeli economy—Gaza is, quite literally, the largest prison on earth, as the British ambassador to Israel pointed out in April 2002. The coming and going of the Jewish colonists (and any number of other arbitrary excuses) is used as a rationale for turning on and off the circulation of Palestinians among their own towns, unpredictably keeping workers away from their meager jobs—though unemployment in Gaza is reaching 70 percent in any case. Children are separated from their schools, parents from their children, farmers from what's left of their crops, and patients from the hospitals meant to serve them. A significant number of Palestinians have died at these checkpoints, forbidden, at the slightest whim of the Israeli guards, from reaching emergency rooms.

All of this leaves out, of course, the devastating violence regularly and sadistically visited on the hapless inhabitants of the West Bank and Gaza by the Israeli army and air force, whose frequent assaults and bombardments exhibit a wanton disregard for human life. It likewise omits the ongoing demolition of houses (over a thousand Palestinian homes have been deliberately demolished by the Israelis since 2000, on top of the thousands of Palestinian homes that Israel has systematically destroyed since 1967). It also neglects the mass arrests and detentions, the destruction of trees and crops, and the gratuitous misery produced as a result.[12] Various international organizations have been warning of the dramatic deterioration in living standards among the already brutalized Palestinian population—two-thirds of whom, according to a recent World Bank report, now live on less than two dollars a day—left increasingly dependent on relief handouts. Palestinian children already exhibit growing symptoms of malnutrition, according to the United States Agency for International Development. Men, women, and children alike are facing an uncertain future of continued confinement, harassment, dismemberment, and death—this, for no other reason than that they had the misfortune of having been born Palestinian on land that a restless, voracious enemy seeks to control at any cost.

And things seem set to get worse before they get any better. The Israelis have started plowing a new barrier through the West Bank. Unequivocally

12. See the report by the United Nations Relief and Works Agency, 10 May 2004, http://domino.un.org/unrwa/index.html

condemned by the International Court of Justice in The Hague as well as the General Assembly of the United Nations—nothing that has ever stopped the Israelis or given any pause to their supporters in the United States—the barrier will ultimately be 420 miles in length. The concrete sections of the barrier already built in the northern West Bank are eight meters high, twice the height of the Berlin Wall, and surrounded on either side by one hundred meters of buffer zones, electric fences, watchtowers, machine-gun emplacements, cameras, and sensors. "A $2 billion installation," Jeff Halper points out, "it is not designed to be dismantled."[13] Rather than following the edge of the West Bank, the barrier runs far into what was supposed to have been Palestinian territory and, even after various modifications imposed by the Israeli high court, it will end up annexing in effect about half of the West Bank. It will do so, however, in order to tie the Israeli colonies into Israel proper; as a result, the Palestinian areas will be even further split into smaller and smaller enclaves and "security zones." In some cases, Palestinian communities will find themselves—indeed, many already have—cut off from the rest of the West Bank, wedged between the separation wall and Israel proper, and hence in military "closed areas" from which residents can be summarily expelled at any time. In the first phase of construction alone, sixteen Palestinian towns find themselves in such circumstances; some fifty other towns have been cut off from their farmland, much of which has, in any case, been bulldozed to make room for the wall (already, some four thousand acres of fertile land have been razed and a hundred thousand trees uprooted just to clear space for it). In other cases, such as the town of Qalqilya, home to tens of thousands of people, Palestinian communities will be entirely surrounded by the wall, cut off from farmland, pastures, markets, and the rest of the world, entirely at the mercy of Israel. The impact on the local economy, which has become ever more dependent on agriculture, will be catastrophic. Israel's thirst for cheap labor, once fulfilled by Palestinians from the Occupied Territories, is now entirely satisfied by the transient and much more tractable human resources provided by the global labor market, principally from Southeast Asia and eastern Europe. In the heavily affected area around Tulkarm, for example, the unemployment rate ballooned from 18 percent to 78 percent after the wall went up.

This barrier represents three simultaneous desires on the part of Israel. First, it obviously gives physical form to Israel's territorial and biopolitical aspirations on the West Bank. By absorbing most of the Jewish colonies—whose dispersal was intended all along to make it difficult to integrate them

---

13. Jeff Halper, "Beyond Road Maps and Walls," *Link* 37 (Jan.–Mar. 2004): 5; and see http://www.ameu.org/page.asp?iid = 255&aid = 390

into Israel proper without catastrophically disrupting the Palestinian communities among which they had been forcibly embedded—the Israelis will, as I said, end up annexing about half of the West Bank. With the consolidation of the West Bank colonies, Gaza can be easily and painlessly renounced. "The confinement of one and a half million persons in a huge holding pen," as Benvenisti has noted, "fulfills the ideal of putting an end to the occupation, and furnishes some relief about how 'we are not responsible'" ("FBS"). Second, the combination of the wall and the expansive network of bypass roads as well as the grid of roadblocks and checkpoints will permanently disable Palestinian life on the West Bank. Literally penned like animals into tiny enclaves cut off from one another and from the rest of the universe, the Palestinians will finally find life—difficult as it has been over the last thirty years—totally impossible. And that is precisely the point; by making their lives impossible, the Israelis hope to induce as many Palestinians as possible to give up and go away. The third point, then, is that the wall represents Israel's desire to fulfill Zionism's greatest dream and, finally, do away with the Palestinians, if not by outright massacre or explicit transfer then by bludgeoning them into a subhuman, animal-like irrelevance—precisely what has happened to the hapless inhabitants of Gaza, whose lives are now wasting away in the gigantic concentration camp the Israelis have built for them.

With some notable exceptions, advocates of the mainstream peace movement in Israel generally remain committed to the agenda set at Oslo. Dismayed by the stall in the peace process, all they want is to go back to the negotiating table within the same set of parameters invented by Rabin, which give the comforting illusion that there really is a chance of peace through separation and apartheid. Witness the two most recent alternatives to the apartheid wall, the Nusseibeh-Ayalon agreement and the so-called Geneva accord. Though both pacts have been heralded as promising alternatives to Sharon's apartheid wall, they represent nothing new. In each case the Palestinian side has yielded the right of return and much else besides in exchange for little more than the same old promises handed out at Oslo: a statelet with carefully selected "attributes of sovereignty" (to use the language of the Bush "road map"); no control over borders, airspace, resources, or water; no dismantling of the colonies; and no Israeli recognition of the historic wrongs committed by the Zionists in 1948—and, hence, no real redress for the Palestinian refugees, who lost their world in what they call the *nakba*, or catastrophe, of that year (see "GB").

In fact, the soft-core Israeli position, as expressed in the Geneva accord or in the inconsequential offerings of Daniel Ayalon (who, like the negotiators at Geneva, has no status in the Israeli government anyway), is at heart little better than the more honest, hard-core position taken by Sharon. While it at least offers nominal recognition to the Palestinians, it does so on the basis that they must remain in the role of the other to the Jewish self of Israel. In other words, the soft-core Zionist position merely perpetuates the racial and colonial mind-set with which the earliest Zionists set out from Europe and thus leaves intact the self/other dichotomy that fuels political Zionism. This is why various analysts, including Israelis such as Pappé, recognize that separation is really domination—"'Separation' is a means to oppress and dominate," as Benvenisti puts it ("FBS")—and that peace proposals based on the logic of demographic separation merely perpetuate the basis of the struggle rather than meaningfully address it. "The flaw at the heart of all such initiatives, the clear evidence that they are destined not to lead to any real peace," writes Azmi Beshara, "is that they are rooted in a process of separation made necessary by the demand to maintain a large Jewish majority in the Israeli political entity."[14]

Take, as representative of this soft-core Zionism, the effusive article that Amos Oz, recognized as one of Israel's leading "doves," published recently in the *Los Angeles Times*. In the article, Oz celebrates the Geneva accord because it demonstrates, according to him, that both sides are willing to give up their dreams—the Israelis the dream of a greater Israel, and the Palestinians the dream of a greater Palestine. In return, he says, the Israelis get to hold on to the purely Jewish state of their dreams, and the Palestinians get a little state of their very own. It should be obvious by now what is wrong with this position. Oz is, first of all, equating the dream of a "greater" Israel with that of a "Greater Palestine"—but there is no such dream. Second, Oz is making it seem that an equal sacrifice would be taking place here: the Israelis would give up their illegal and brutal colonization of the West Bank, Gaza, and Jerusalem, and, in exchange, the Palestinians would give up their historical claim to their homeland, from which they were violently expelled by a marauding colonial army. In equating these sacrifices, Oz is equating the Zionist dream of a purely Jewish state with the Palestinian dream of a free Palestine.

This is where the true problem lies. What Israelis like Oz want to cling to at all costs is their dream of a purely Jewish state, but, for their part, the Palestinians as a whole do not call for a purely *non-Jewish* state. Historically, in fact, Palestine always had a thriving native Jewish population; Palestine has indeed always historically represented plurality and heterogeneity. So we see a disequilibrium here between, on the one hand, a dream of an ex-

14. Beshara, "A Short History of Apartheid."

clusive and exclusionary state and, on the other hand, a dream of a democratic and secular and, hence, *inclusive* state. This, incidentally, was the declared Palestinian objective as far back as the Palestine National Charter of 1964—which a string of U.S. and Israeli governments have insisted that the Palestinians renounce.[15]

We have come, then, to the heart of the matter. For one thing, Israel is not now, nor can it ever be, a purely Jewish state as long as 20 percent (at least) of the population is non-Jewish. To be more precise, the presence of those non-Jews—the Israeli Palestinians—will continue to pose an insurmountable philosophical and political conundrum for a state that wants (according to its ethnotheological fantasy of itself) to pretend to be both Jewish and democratic but, in fact, ends up being neither one nor the other. What, then, the soft-core Oz has in common with the hard-core Sharon—where the soft-liberal Zionism meets its violent alter ego—is that both seek at all costs (to the Palestinians) to preserve the fantasy of a purely Jewish state. For Sharon's plan, according to Benvenisti, "appears to promise the existence of a 'Jewish democratic state' via 'separation,' 'the end of the conquest,' the 'dismantling of settlements'—and also the imprisonment of some three million Palestinians in Bantustans. This is an 'interim plan' which is meant to last forever." But, Benvenisti adds, "the plan will last, however, only as long as the illusion that 'separation' is a means to end the dispute is sustained" ("FBS"). Benvenisti's larger point is that such an approach—apartheid—is doomed in the long run. However, by having rendered totally impossible the constitution of a viable independent Palestinian state, Sharon will have (unwittingly) laid the ground for the integration of both peoples, Palestinians and Israelis, into one political entity, one state: Zionism's nightmare scenario.

We have, in any case, run out of alternatives. The two-state solution that the Palestinian leadership embraced in 1988—fifteen years and thousands of lives ago—is ultimately not really workable; it probably never really was. The facts on the ground that the Israelis rushed to accomplish over the last fifteen years—the colonies; the bypass road network; the apartheid wall; the systematic uprooting and destruction of the basis of Palestinian existence, its water wells, orchards, factories, workshops, trees, houses, ancient olive groves, farmland, pasture; and the thousands upon thousands of innocent human lives that Zionism has exacted from its victims in return for its un-

---

15. The closest one can come to the ideological violence of Zionism among the Palestinians is the reactive phenomenon of suicide bombing, which, however, came into being only under the extreme pressures of an occupation that has crushed virtually all other forms of Palestinian political expression.

quenchable ethnic, racial, religious, and colonial ambitions—there is no undoing of all these things.

Halper, Pappé, Benvenisti, and many other Israelis—as well as Palestinians such as Beshara—now recognize that, in the end, the only possible solution to the question of Palestine is a single state. In calling for the constitution of a single state between the Jordan River and the Mediterranean (which Halper, for his part, envisions as the first stage in the formation of a wider Middle East Union), Pappé eloquently warns of the dangers posed not only by the segregationist Geneva accord but by the fantasy that it prompted among liberal Israelis that Tel Aviv could one day become the Geneva of the Middle East. "Tel Aviv is not Geneva," Pappé writes; "it is built on the ruins of six Palestinian villages destroyed in 1948; and it shouldn't be Geneva: it should aspire to be Alexandria or Beirut, so that Jews who invaded the Arab world by force could at last show a willingness to be part of the Middle East rather than remain an alien and alienated state within it" ("GB").

A single state for both Israelis and Palestinians is, of course, what Edward Said himself worked and argued for throughout the final years of his life, the inevitable conclusion of his humanism and his interest in the idea of Palestine: "Two people in one land. Or, equality for all. Or, one person one vote. Or a common humanity asserted in a binational state."[16] Pointing out that, on the one hand, Israel will never (bar the completion of the ethnic cleansing of 1948) be the purely Jewish state of Zionism's dreams and that, on the other hand, Palestinian self-determination in a separate state is unworkable, Said argued that the real question is not how to devise means to separate the two populations but "to see whether it is possible for them to live together as fairly and peacefully as possible." There are, Said argued, not only Palestinians but also

> Israeli Jews today who speak candidly about "post-Zionism," insofar as, after 50 years of Israeli history, classic Zionism has neither provided a solution to the Palestinian presence, nor an exclusively Jewish presence. I see no other way than to begin now to speak about sharing the land that has thrust us together, sharing it in a truly democratic way, with equal rights for each citizen. There can be no reconciliation unless both peoples, two communities of suffering, resolve that their existence is a secular fact, and that it has to be dealt with as such.[17]

Ultimately, indeed, and especially—but not only—in the hands of Said, the Palestinian struggle against Zionism, as it has evolved over the past few

16. Said, "The Only Alternative," *Al-Ahram Weekly*, 1-7 Mar. 2001.
17. Said, "Truth and Reconciliation."

decades, represents not merely a nationalist struggle of the classical variety but, rather, the will to negate the exclusivism of Zionism and replace it with something else—that humanist alternative—which Israelis like Pappé *also* yearn for: integration, cooperation, sharing, belonging, being in common. Zionism as we have come to know it, the Israeli historian Gabriel Piterberg points out, is inherently and constitutionally incompatible with Arab-Jewish cooperation; in opposing and refusing the violent alterity of Zionism, what the idea of Palestine proposes is the hope of a cooperative sharing. This sense of an alternative, shared, and cooperative future is precisely what Said had in mind whenever he evoked the idea of Palestine.

The idea of Palestine, thus, reflects to Zionism not the distorted mirror image of its own antagonism and violence but, instead, a humanism of liberation, a humanism that would free Jews as well as Arabs. "Maybe time is running out," an interviewer once suggested to Said, who replied, "We fight on. And we keep saying, 'We're going to live together with you.'" He added, "No matter what they do, we're a shadow." What Said is articulating here is the idea of Palestine as a kind of shadow to the violent alterity of Zionism. The idea of Palestine here expresses the logic of a fully anticolonial humanism of liberation, a will that the traumatic encounter of colonizer and colonized, occupier and occupied, self and other, which has historically been essential to Zionism, could be overcome by an affirmation of unity rather than division, sharing rather than denial.

Secular Divination: Edward Said's Humanism

W. J. T. Mitchell

Humanism . . . engenders its own opposite.
—Edward Said, *Beginnings* (1975)[1]

Any continuation of the conversation with Edward Said would have to include the question of humanism and its many discontents. Humanism for Said was always a dialectical concept, generating oppositions it could neither absorb nor avoid. The very word used to cause in him mixed feelings of reverence and revulsion: an admiration for the great monuments of civilization that constitute the archive of humanism and a disgust at humanism's underside of suffering and oppression that, as Benjamin insisted, make them monuments to barbarism as well. Said's last book, *Humanism and Democratic Criticism,* is, among other things, his attempt to trace the evolution of his own thinking from his training as an academic humanist in the philological tradition of Auerbach and Spitzer, through the antihumanist period of French theory in the U.S. academy since the sixties, to the present moment of posthumanism, when humanism looks to many like a dead issue, not even requiring or generating an interesting opposition any more (unless the posthuman is to be understood as a dialectic moment of humanism rather than some irrevocable cancellation of it).[2] Said was perhaps uniquely situated to trace this process because he, among all the academic intellectuals of the sixties and seventies generation, seemed to simultaneously absorb and resist the arrival of antihumanism in the form of what is loosely called French theory. Said's engagement with Foucault in *Beginnings* and *Orientalism* was persistent and deep, leading James Clifford

---

1. Edward W. Said, *Beginnings: Intention and Method* (1975; New York, 2004), p. 373.
This paper was first composed for a colloquium at Columbia University on the occasion of the publication of *Humanism and Democratic Criticism,* 27 April 2004.
2. See Said, *Humanism and Democratic Criticism* (New York, 2004), p. 10; hereafter abbreviated *HDC.*

to question whether it was possible for Said to continue to profess allegiance to humanism, with its assumptions of subjective agency and will, while embracing the antihumanist tendencies of structuralism and poststructuralism.

Said's answer to Clifford is, quite simply, yes: "it is possible to be critical of humanism in the name of humanism" and, perhaps even more emphatically, it is *necessary* to be critical of humanism in order to be worthy of the name (*HDC*, p. 10). Humanism shows a double face. It is, on the one hand, the capacious learning, the extended intelligence (what Bourdieu, quoted by Said, calls the "collective intellectual") that provides the materials and archives for human self-knowledge, but, on the other hand, it can be a stuffy, sterile antiquarianism, a sentimental, hollow piety about the human, a development that has in turn produced various shallow antihumanisms and posthumanisms. Said wants to reclaim and revivify humanism for our time, to link the work of academics with the precedent of Auerbach (on the side of learning) but also with criticism and the precedent of Fanon and Trilling—the moment of choice, decision, taking of sides, judgment. Without criticism, humanism remains a sterile fever for the archive as a dynastic treasure and an end in itself. Without humanism, criticism is nothing but empty quibbling and opinion.

So where does this leave the issue of democracy? This, I think, is precisely the space, both real and utopian, in which humanism and criticism make their connection. Said knows very well that *democracy* is (like the niggling, fussy irrelevance of criticism and the musty tomes of the humanists) a hollow term, too often used as a cover for imperialist adventures (the U.S. is, after all, currently trying to bring democracy to Iraq by military force). The language of democracy, of equality, of power sharing, of justice, of secular self-governance must not be co-opted by ideologues but must be reclaimed and reinfused with practical meaning for human relationships. And a democracy is, if it is anything, a place where power grows out of arguments, knowledge, language, persuasion, and reason—in short, out of the resources made available by humanism and criticism. Democratic criticism, then, means not only the right to dissent but the obligation to dissent, to break one's silence and passivity, to "speak the truth to power" without fear of censorship or violence. Humanism is what gives the critic something to say. Criticism is what gives the humanist a motive, occasion, and obligation to say something. And democracy is the space in which knowledge and

W. J. T. MITCHELL is the Gaylord Donnelley Distinguished Service Professor of English and art history at the University of Chicago and editor of *Critical Inquiry*. His latest book, *What Do Pictures Want?* will appear in 2005.

judgment, learning and dissent, come together. It is the space that allows for this convergence, whether in the sphere of politics and society or in the smaller world of academic discussion, right down to the democratic classroom. It is also the space *created by* this convergence, the (relatively) noncoercive or at least nonviolent realm of the free play of ideas and imagination that is never perfectly realized but always approached as the goal of discourse.

Said's great enemies, then, are never merely political, but intellectual, cultural, and academic: the tendency to obfuscation and mystification; the cult of expertise, whether in academic jargon or in the prattlings of the policy wonks; the countercult of false transparency in the oversimplified sound bites of the punditocracy; the simplistic binarisms of the "clash of civilizations" thesis, the "axis of evil"; and the reductionism of mass media "information." And his allies: complexity without mystification, dialectics without the disabling equivocation of ambivalence or deconstructive "undecidability" (*HDC*, p. 66), recognition of the baffling limits of human knowledge without obscurantism or quietism; and a recognition of the situatedness and contingency of every utterance without a surrender to relativism and without a sacrifice of abiding principles. Sooner pass a camel through the eye of the needle than come up to the unbelievably demanding standards Said set for intellectual expression. No wonder that the transcendent standard above all this is a term that (so far as I can recall) he never invokes in *Humanism and Democratic Criticism* but that informs all his work, and that is *virtuosity,* an agile, improvisational sense of balance coupled with a dogged and tireless preparation for the next moment of struggle.

I do not know how this book will be remembered and compared with his other great works. My favorites are still *Beginnings, Orientalism,* and *After the Last Sky,* his marvelous collaboration with the Swiss photographer Jean Mohr in an effort to "represent" the Palestinians to themselves and to the world. But this book strikes me as a distillation of what Said called his late style, informal, freely ruminative, personal, and tirelessly reexamining his thinking as it encountered the new circumstances of the post-9/11 world. It is a performance of exactly the convergence of the humanistic with the critical and the democratic that his title promises. Critical of humanism and humanists, humane in the motivations of its criticism, and relentlessly critical of the world's most powerful democracy, its delusions and its promises, this is a worthy testament, a kind of farewell letter to Edward's devoted, diverse, and always contentious following.

In Edward's own spirit, then, I would like to raise a question that has always nagged me throughout his work, and that is his division of the secular from the sacred. This is an absolutely foundational distinction for Said, and in some versions of it I see a problem that remains unresolved. Here is the formulation in *Humanism and Democratic Criticism:*

> the core of humanism is the secular notion that the historical world is made by men and women, and not by God, and that it can be understood rationally according the principle formulated by Vico in *New Science,* that we can really know only what we make or, to put it differently, we can know things according to the way they were made. [*HDC*, p. 11]

Vico's scientific humanism, as formulated by Said, contains the implicit suggestion that we *cannot* know things that we have not made. This leads then to the notion that religious knowledge, sacred knowledge, is really a kind of ignorance or at least an unscientific and even inhuman form of knowledge. This would presumably be the case whether religious knowledge expressed itself by a kind of confession of ignorance and uncertainty or, conversely, by an assertion of dogma based in faith. Either way, *sacred knowledge* is a kind of oxymoron and has no claim to share in the progressive, open, dialogical, and (ultimately) democratic ethos that Said associates with humanism.

There is also a further implication in Viconian humanism and that is the question of the scientific knowledge of nature. If the Viconian postulate is taken at face value, human beings should not be able to have rational knowledge of nature because they did not create it. Only human nature, and specifically human history, are open to rational understanding.

> The world of civil society has certainly been made by men, and . . . its principles are therefore to be found within the modifications of our own human mind. Whoever reflects on this cannot but marvel that the philosophers should have been putting all their energies to the study of the world of nature, which, since God made it, He alone knows; and that they should have neglected the study of the world of nations, or civil world, which, since men had made it, men could come to know.[3]

The natural and supernatural realms are both closed to rational inquiry of the sort distinctive to humanism. This seems like an obvious problem, especially on the side of the natural sciences, which are generally taken to be accessible to rational, open, empirical, and even democratically progressive forms of knowledge. Humanistic knowledge is generally taken to be a poor relation of natural science when it comes to precision and certainty. If anything, natural science is a kind of model for what secular hu-

---

3. Giambattista Vico, *The New Science,* in *The Rise of Modern Mythology, 1680–1860,* ed. Burton Feldman and Robert D. Richardson (Bloomington, Ind., 1972), p. 57.

manism might aspire to. Said admits as much when he praises Darwin's "lifelong attention to the lowly earthworm revealed [in] its capacity for expressing nature's variability and design without necessarily seeing the whole of either one or the other," and thus, in Adam Phillips's words (quoted by Said), "replacing 'a creation myth with a secular maintenance myth'" (*HDC*, pp. 140–41).

One can hear the resonance of Said's distinction between "origin myths" and "beginnings" echoing in this passage. Beginnings are provisional, historically situated actions, decisions, and choices, not reified, timeless moments prior to human agency. They do not have the absoluteness or certainty of creation ex nihilo but are provisional origins that could turn out to be dead ends or the start of something big. Beginnings are also connected immediately with acts of continuation (or of turning, swerving aside) and not with some predestined fate or necessity. As such, they perfectly negotiate the dilemma of agency versus external determination that Clifford criticized in Said's Foucauldian work, where he seemed not to have worked out the relation between his humanistic emphasis on freedom and agency and Foucault's antihumanistic determinism.[4] Is not a "secular maintenance myth," epitomized by the blind labors of the earthworm, exactly a figure of the refusal to choose between these false alternatives, and is not Darwin himself implicitly a kind of earthworm in his patient, tireless work, in which both the lowest and the highest forms of knowledge must be combined?

I am not primarily concerned here with pointing up the obvious problem in Vico's epistemology that this example illustrates. The notion that we can only have rational knowledge of what we have made is clearly wrong, but the sphere of natural science is not really the focus of Said's insistence on the secular character of humanism. (Also, to be precise about Vico, his view was that scientific knowledge actually *is* a human creation insofar as experimental research must imitate the processes of nature, reproduce them under artificial conditions that make them accessible to knowledge; in that sense, natural science *is* a form of knowledge of human productions. What we know in natural science is not nature in any direct sense but a second nature fabricated in the laboratory.)

But it is the domain of religion that Said so often characterizes in terms of fairly reductive stereotypes: dogmatic, fanatical, irrational, intolerant, and obsessed with mystery, obfuscation, and human helplessness in the

---

4. See James Clifford, "On *Orientalism*," *The Predicament of Culture: Twentieth-Century Ethnography, Literature, and Art* (Cambridge, Mass., 1988), pp. 255–76. See also Akeel Bilgrami's excellent preface to *HDC*, p. xii.

presence of the inscrutable divine (or demonic) design. "Religious enthu-siasm is perhaps the most dangerous of threats to the humanistic enterprise, since it is patently antisecular and antidemocratic in nature" (*HDC*, p. 51). If natural science turns human beings into objects buffeted by impersonal, nonhuman forces, religion does the same thing, only with the added prob-lem of mystery, irrationality, and dogma, accompanied by authoritarian in-stitutions and radically undemocratic, coercive practices. At least the forces of nature can be understood and to some extent controlled by human agency; the divine, in Said's lexicon, seems to be exactly that sphere of the uncontrollable and inexplicable that, at the same time, has an immense power over human thought and action. Religion for Said is an expression of the alienated capacities of the human imagination, a system of ideological deception and coercive authority.

I bring this up as an issue because it strikes me as a limitation in Said's thinking that he often transcended in practice but (so far as I know) never at the level of theoretical reflection. It leads me to the point where I think of Said's work as intersecting most directly with my own and yet where I often felt the greatest distance between our ways of thinking. This point is not really any single issue, but it does revolve around questions of religion and mystery, on the one hand, and problems of mass culture, media, and (for lack of a better word) images, or imagination, or the visual, on the other, as Edward's self-confessed blind spot, the domain of visual art that left him frequently baffled or panicky. Said's aesthetic polestars were music and lit-erature, two great orders of art that to him were much more than mere cultural ornaments or diversions, but exemplars of human possibility in its most ambitious moments. Literature, of course, for Said included not only fiction, poetry, and dramatic writing, but the nonfiction prose, the "critical" writing, and the philological learning that lay behind them. Philology for Said was the love of words quite literally, a love that treated words, not as mere instruments for polemic or analysis, but as living presences that an-imate discourse with passion, eloquence, and exactly that form of self-knowledge and self-criticism that makes humanism worthy of its name. He rejected the divisions among writers and scholars and critics and tried to fuse the vocations of all three—creativity, learning, and judgment—in the role of that rarest of creatures in American culture, the public intellectual.

As for music, my sense is that this is where Said's identity as a formalist, an aesthete, and a high modernist intellectual is most firmly located. His role as a talented amateur musician perfectly exemplified his refusal of spe-cialization, on the one hand, while his writing on music in the tradition of Adorno carried him well beyond any taint of amateurism into the virtuosic company of Barenboim, Glenn Gould, and others. Beyond this, music had for him a kind of analogical significance in his insistence on translating the abstruse turnings of dialectical reasonings into a style of contrapuntal critical writing, a prose that continually played multiple countermelodies against the main line of his thought, qualifying, intersecting, correcting, and elaborating in surprising new forms. Above all is his sense of what Wordsworth called "the still sad music of humanity," never more movingly expressed than in his sense of the final unity of two peoples separated by savage violence, the Israelis and the Palestinians, whose intertwined, contrapuntal relationship he compared to a "tragic symphony."[5]

What, then, of the visual arts? I interviewed him on this subject for a special issue of *Boundary 2* in 2001 and encountered a strange, unusual diffidence in Said's approach to the subject. After noting his "highly developed vocabulary" for talking about "the auditory and the verbal," he confessed himself to be "tongue-tied" with the visual arts: "just to think about the visual arts generally sends me into a panic." Of course this turned out to be only a momentary perplexity, and Said quickly regained his balance, talking with considerable eloquence about a range of visual artworks from masters of painting, such as El Greco, Goya, and Picasso, to his childhood memories of the wax museum of Egyptian history in Cairo and the anatomical representations of human diseases in the Agriculture Museum of Giza. The consistent form this eloquence took, however, was a registering of the "haunted" and "frightening" character of the religious images, the terrified fascination that the medical images produced, and (most centrally) the deformed bodies of El Greco, Francis Bacon, and Goya, with their lurid colors and scenes of monstrous disfiguration. Of all the artists we discussed, Edward felt the most affinity for Goya whose combination of detached irony, passionate involvement, and "a kind of gentleness in the middle of all the violence" impressed him like no other painter.[6]

I would like to suggest a link, however speculative and impressionistic, between Said's "panic" with images and visual representations with what Lacan (whom I am pretty sure Edward mainly disliked) would have called the Imaginary, and with one of the most characteristic gestures of Said's writing; that is, the moment of "bafflement" or mystification, of coming to the limits of his thought and recognizing that encounter in his own discourse. This is of course a familiar rhetorical trope (perhaps a form of *occupatio*, the saying of what cannot or will not be said), but it is also a deeply

---

5. Said, "My Right of Return," *Power, Politics, and Culture: Interviews with Edward Said*, ed. Gauri Viswanathan (New York, 2001), p. 447.

6. Said, "The Panic of the Visual: A Conversation with Edward W. Said," interview with Mitchell, in *Edward Said and the Work of the Critic: Speaking Truth to Power*, ed. Paul Bové (Durham, N.C., 2000), pp. 31, 34, 33.

ethical gesture, a kind of deferral of authority, a public confession of uncertainty.

I want to see this as Said's gesture toward the limits of his thought and
link them to his deep involvement with similar issues in Vico. For Vico, the
image, the imaginary (whether visual or verbal, picture or metaphor) is the
expressive mode of primitive man immersed in the realm of fantasy, idols,
animism, personification, and vivid poetic figures. It is the language of religion and myth—not, however, the language of *revealed* religion ("the Hebrew religion was founded by the true God on the prohibition of the
divination on which all the gentile nations arose").[7] Judaism, like other religions of the book, is grounded on a prohibition of idols, images, and divination. Vico is talking about pagan religions of icons, fetishes, not the
religions of the book. The interesting twist here is that Vico's concept of the
secular rests on, and grows out of, the mythologies of the gentiles, not out
of revealed religion. More precisely, the history of civil society, of the gentiles
and nations, is the *subject* of Vico's new science, while its epistemological
foundations lie outside that subject, in the unquestioned (and tactfully unexamined) dogmas of "true" (that is, revealed) religion. Vico's notion of a
secular history is framed inside a providential, yet tragic cycle: men begin
as bestial savages, develop gods out of their projected fantasies based in a
fear of nature, and grow toward gradual refinement, to civilization, and,
finally, to decadence produced by skepticism. Thus, Vico says that the revealed religion of the Jews was grounded on "the prohibition of divination,"
which is fundamentally the second commandment, the prohibition on
graven images.[8] But this means that the distinction between the sacred and
secular is not quite so clean as it might seem; it is actually more like the
difference between direct access to the divine word and divination of sacred
images. But this requires a modification in Vico's sense of where human
knowledge can attain most clarity. For the sacred images that are created by
men, the idols that mystify them, are precisely what eludes their understanding. Divination of idols or other symbols is, from the point of view of
revealed religion, nothing but magical, superstitious ritual, the false attri-
bution of intentions and desires to inanimate objects and images. Insofar
as secular knowledge is to be distinguished from revealed religion, then, it
is much *less* certain about its claims, necessarily provisional and hypothet-
ical. It is, in fact, grounded in divination rather than revelation, and the
genealogy of the secular goes deeper than the Enlightenment, reaching back

7. Vico, *The New Science*, p. 56.
8. For the link between the prohibition on divination and the second commandment, see
Moshe Halbertal and Avishai Margalit, *Idolatry* (Cambridge, Mass., 1992), pp. 105–6.

into pagan origins. Divination might be seen, paradoxically, as a distinctly *secular* hermeneutics in contrast to the sacred hermeneutic tradition grounded in the Bible. Divination is associated with the interpretation of human and natural objects—auguries based in the material body and its states, prophecies based in the formal alignments of stars or the behavior of animals, or diagnoses based in the analysis of dreams and (most notably) in graven images and works of art.

The strange lineage of the sacred/secular distinction in Vico, then, is I think one explanation for Said's frequent recourse to the language of uncertainty, paradox, irresolution, and what he calls bafflement in his writings. Bafflement is associated with unresolved contradictions, mysterious, labyrinthine forms, the "magic" of words, the encounter with what Leo Spitzer called "the inward life center" of the work of art. And of course there is Said's almost structural distaste for religion and myth, as opposed to his secular or "rational civil theology,"[9] the phrase that Vico uses to describe his own position. Like Vico, Said wants to see all these myths and images as human productions, therefore accessible to rational understanding, because they are man-made in the first place. But to inhabit a regime of these images is precisely to be beset by the irrational, by the mysterious forces of the alienated productions of the human imagination—the "tyrannical feedback system" that Said found diagnosed and (he hoped) resisted in the work of Foucault.[10] Suppose Vico's deeper lesson was that human beings finally cannot sustain a knowledge/power relation to their own creations but find themselves caught up as victims in the terrible systems (social, economic, and political) that they have wrought. This is the strange, melancholy lesson of *The New Science*. Vico's tragic narrative tells us that man only emerges briefly (during the age of man) from the age of gods and heroes before sinking back into savagery with the rise of skepticism and the resurgence of superstition. This narrative helps to clarify why Said was so antagonistic to deconstruction, posthumanism, and antifoundationalism, why refined, technical academic discourse was so grating on his ears. It was part of his resistance to decadence and decline, his insistence on the intellectual's responsibility to lost causes and unfashionable ideas (humanism, criticism), and his wariness about hollow ideals (democracy) used in the service of domination.

Vico's "rational civil theology" is the best name for Edward Said's religion of reading and writing, humanism and democratic criticism. It is, however, a rationality that collides routinely with the irrational products of the hu-

---

9. Vico summarizes his own humanism with this phrase. See Vico, *The New Science*, p. 54.
10. Said, *Beginnings*, p. 288.

man imagination, the cultural, social, and political creations that should be intelligible because they are human creations but that continually elude that understanding, whether they are the heroic products of artistic volition or alienated structures such as the unconscious, colonialism, or capital. Early on in his career, Edward rejected the "uncanny" criticism of Hillis Miller and the Yale school because he thought it gave in too easily and revelled in the irrational, undecidable character of arts and letters. But it is clear that his own brand of canny, secular criticism is devised precisely as a form of resistance to an uncanny element in the objects of study—the productions of the human mind. Part of his canniness was to recognize his own work as a kind of interpretive lost cause that would continually founder on the object of its study. Let us call it by the name of secular divination, an oxymoron that Vico and Said would have understood. Like all the other lost causes that Said pursued, this one gave his writing that bracing sense of clarity, resolute determination, and tragic pathos that was the distinctive feature of his style, both early and late.

Global Comparativism

Aamir R. Mufti

It is famously (and perhaps notoriously) the case that in his major works at least, Edward Said seems to be concerned chiefly, if not entirely, with the canonical literatures of the modern West, either bracketing off the cultural production and trajectories of non-Western societies or bringing to them modes of attention distinct from, and far less compelling than, those he has developed for a critical reengagement with the Western tradition. This appears to be especially true of literatures produced in languages of non-Western origin. I claim that elements of a consideration of the conditions under which such literatures may and must be brought into the purview of contemporary humanistic knowledge are present in relatively developed form in his work. It may even be argued that a concern with these languages and literatures, especially of course Arabic, and their place in literary studies animates his work even when its explicit preoccupation appears to be elsewhere. It is my goal to point to some of these elements and suggest a number of ways in which they may be put into articulation. My larger concern, whose fuller elaboration must be postponed for another occasion, is to reopen the old question of what I shall call the *Eurocentrism* of the knowledge structures we inhabit, a question of enormous significance facing the hu-

Versions of this essay were presented at UCLA, Nanjing University, and the Bibliothèque Nationale in Paris. I am deeply grateful to Fred Jameson, Kirstie McClure, Gabi Piterberg, Vince Pecora, Paul Bové, Joe Buttigieg, Ronald Judy, Akeel Bilgrami, Pascale Casanova, Lindsay Waters, Q. S. Tong, and Efrain Kristal for their questions, objections, and calls for clarification on those occasions and elsewhere. The present version has benefited enormously from their input, which I acknowledge here collectively. My ideas here have also been influenced in important ways by my teaching experience at UCLA during 2003–4 in two graduate seminars. I am grateful to my students in those seminars for being the testing ground for these ideas and also significant interlocutors.

manities today but one whose serious exploration is tripped up by its easy insertion into a polemical mode.

The suggestions offered here are part of an ongoing discussion with colleagues and students, at my institution and elsewhere, about the need for and possibilities of discovering ways of making the humanities respond more adequately to the hierarchical situation of global culture, a kind of response that Gayatri Spivak, in her recent book on the situation of comparative literature, *Death of a Discipline,* has dubbed evocatively "planetarity."[1] They are also an attempt to take a step further, discussions I had had with Said himself on numerous occasions over the final years of his life. As a student of his in the late 1980s and early 1990s, I had been witness at close hand to his attempt in *Culture and Imperialism* to address what I believe he took to be the most disturbing critique of *Orientalism,* namely, that his critique of the Eurocentrism of the humanities appeared to center almost exclusively on this same European culture. The concept of contrapuntality, which called for a whole new way of reading and even of positioning oneself in the world, was in part an attempt to respond to this critique. Since leaving Columbia University in the mid-1990s, I have attempted in my work in various ways to engage with certain aspects of Said's oeuvre, to pick up where he seemed to have left off, to pursue directions that were only hinted at in his works, or to explore possibilities that were implicit in them. These remarks are a continuation of that work and an attempt to imagine what the next conversation with him might have looked like had his long and persistent illness not removed him from our midst in September 2003.

I signify by *Eurocentrism* an *epistemological* problem, too important to be left in the polemical register that seems to have become its fate in contemporary discussion. While, in the present atmosphere, the term cannot be fully denuded of its polemical value, a serious effort in this direction needs nevertheless to be made. As my colleague Shu-mei Shih has recently argued compellingly, we must revisit this question despite the "yawns of familiarity" that it is likely to produce in some circles.[2] I have in mind something like the set of issues Dipesh Chakrabarty points to when he speaks of the stumbling block that he confronts as a historian of India, namely, that

1. See Gayatri Chakravorty Spivak, *Death of a Discipline* (New York, 2003).
2. Shu-mei Shih, "Global Literature and the Technologies of Recognition," *PMLA* 119 (Jan. 2004): 16.

AAMIR R. MUFTI is associate professor of comparative literature at University of California, Los Angeles. He is the editor of "Critical Secularism," a special issue of *Boundary 2* (2004).

something he calls Europe continues to function as "the sovereign, theoretical subject" of all historical knowledge, so that histories that are supposedly "'Indian,' 'Chinese,' [or] 'Kenyan' . . . tend to become variations on
a master narrative that could be called 'the history of Europe.'"[3] From historical periodizations to notions of causality and modes of production narratives, the structures of historical knowledge normalize and *make
normative* the idea of Europe as "the scene of the birth of the modern" (*PE*,
p. 28). In Chakrabarty's reading (of disciplinary history as of "the phenomenal world of everyday relationships of power"), Europe *is* this idea, a "hy-
perreal" term that corresponds not to a geography per se but to "figures of
the imaginary," to modes of identification and organization of cultures (*PE*,
pp. 28, 27). The modes of cultural authority that the idea of Europe regulates
are *Western* in an encompassing sense, underwriting narratives of American
universalism as well as those of a uniquely European polity and culture in
the geographically specific sense.[4] It is the social and cultural *force* of this
idea of Europe in intellectual life, as in the phenomenal world of global
power relations, that I am referring to here as Eurocentrism. Everything in
the present makeup of the humanistic disciplines points toward the conclusion (which is really an *assumption*), mostly implicit but even explicitly
made at certain points, that, as Chakrabarty puts it, "only 'Europe' . . . is
theoretically (that is, at the level of the fundamental categories that shape
historical thinking) knowable; all other histories are matters of empirical
research that fleshes out a theoretical skeleton that is substantially 'Europe'"
(*PE*, p. 29). Humanistic culture is saturated with this informal develop-
mentalism—a "'first in the West, and then elsewhere'" structure of global
time, as Chakrabarty puts it (*PE*, p. 6)—in which cultural objects from non-
Western societies can be grasped only with reference to the categories of
European cultural history, as pale or partial reflections of the latter, to be
seen ultimately as coming late, lagging behind, and lacking in originality.
In literary studies, the problem is symptomatically visible, for instance,
whenever we use the categories of Western literary history—such as romanticism, realism, modernism, or postmodernism—in non-Western contexts (as we constantly do) or of genre to speak of the "Arabic novel" or the
"Urdu short story." It is thus absolutely crucial to acknowledge at the outset
that we are *all* Eurocentric in this sense, even and perhaps especially when
we attempt to tell the story of such non-European objects as Indian, Chinese, and Arabic literature. This acknowledgement is necessary in order

---

3. Dipesh Chakrabarty, *Provincializing Europe: Postcolonial Thought and Historical Difference*
(Princeton, N.J., 2000), p. 27; hereafter abbreviated *PE*.
4. I thank Fred Jameson for suggesting the need for this clarification.

both to recognize the enormity of the problem and the difficulty of effort it requires and to delink this concept, even if partially and for the moment, from its overwhelmingly polemical valence.

I shall move in these remarks between different levels of abstraction, from conceptual clarification to observations about the current state of certain core disciplinary practices, such as language proficiency and the inculcation of what I am calling theory culture—the *habitus* that regulates "theory" as a discrete set of practices within departments of literature—and the ways in which these practices embody Eurocentrism. Requirements structuring the graduate degree in comparative literature will of course be worked out differently by different departments and programs in response to their own institutional histories. But the problem that needs addressing is a shared one across the discipline, namely, that some of the rubrics we have employed over the last decade and a half to compel an encounter between the metropolitan-national formations and the range of alterities they suppress, despite their visible successes, have been unable sufficiently to attend to the forms of cultural otherness that are marked by the non-Western provenance of the languages in which they are produced. Rubrics of critical analysis such as postcolonial literature, minor literatures, world literatures in English, or crossing borders—with which I have myself engaged in various ways—have without doubt helped to facilitate an unlearning of privilege within the dominant cultures, at least in academic and related contexts. So it is out of a long, personal involvement with the practice and development of these modes of analysis and an understanding of their efficacy that I attempt to express my present concern, namely, that they appear to have failed so far to meaningfully include these "other" languages and literatures; they need to be considered as "active cultural media rather than as objects of cultural study," as Spivak has powerfully put it.[5]

We may take as a starting point for this discussion the Bernheimer Report, produced by the American Comparative Literature Association over a decade ago. As the ACLA has convened another committee to update that report, it is time I think for all of us to revisit its recommendations. State of the discipline reports are hardly, by their nature, cutting edge documents or very exciting to read. In the case of this report and the discussion that surrounded it, however, we have a rare instance, with all its limitations, of a genuine and frank disciplinary self-examination, relatively free of bombast and doomsday scenarios. One of the basic emphases of the report and the surrounding discussion was on the question of linguistic competence and the issue of reading literature in the original. The report called on the

---

5. Spivak, *Death of a Discipline*, p. 9.

discipline to mitigate the "old hostilities toward translation" in order to incorporate various "minority" literatures into the curriculum, with a view to the "multicultural recontextualization of Anglo-American and European perspectives." And it recommended with respect to the learning of non-Western languages that students "should be encouraged to broaden their linguistic horizons to encompass at least one non-European language."[6] What exactly we might mean in this context by such terms as "non-Western languages" is of course itself a complex issue, and the report perhaps takes it to be more transparent than it is, for it bears a *historical* solution rather than a philological or civilizational classification.

There is no stable and ultimately satisfying way of distinguishing Western from non-Western, European from non-European in this context, but, very broadly put, I would say that I mean by such designations those varied languages that, in the course of the invention of "Western" culture during the centuries of expansion and domination, have come to be *defined* as external to it. Primarily, of course, this means the languages whose historical origins are in the continental zones of Asia, Africa, and the Americas, and it is the historical experience of these languages and literatures, encompassing masses of humanity and varied and intricate tapestries of cultural experience, that provide, I would argue, our most encompassing paradigms for understanding linguistic and cultural displacement in the modern era. But we should not forget the experience of those language clusters in Eastern Europe and those "minor" languages in the Western countries that have themselves undergone similar processes of marginalization and even decimation. Within comparative literature and the literary humanities more broadly, this hierarchical polarity has its own particular history, and no one today will disagree that, as Wlad Godzich noted some years ago, the origins of the discipline are "firmly Eurocentric" and that "from the outset we have privileged certain literatures, notably the German, French, and English."[7] The tentativeness of the suggestions in the Bernheimer Report hinted already at a partial perception of the untenability of one of the principal linguistic hierarchies that structure the humanistic field, even as they revealed an anxiety about what facing the question squarely would mean for the disciplinary terrain. More than ten years after the writing of the report, however, it remains the case that despite a certain openness toward the in-

6. Charles Bernheimer et al., "The Bernheimer Report, 1993: Comparative Literature at the Turn of the Century," in *Comparative Literature in the Age of Multiculturalism*, ed. Bernheimer (Baltimore, 1995), pp. 44, 43.

7. Wlad Godzich, *The Culture of Literacy* (Cambridge, Mass., 1994), p. 278. A consideration of the vast vistas opened up by Pascale Casanova, *La Republique mondiale des lettres* (Paris, 1999) must of necessity be postponed for another occasion.

clusion of the non-Western languages, these main languages of Western Europe—including, to a lesser degree, Spanish and Italian—remain the core languages of the discipline, and Europe constitutes its only axis of comparison. Many of our departments are now producing students who work mainly on literatures in non-Western languages, and we expect of these students, *or rather should do,* that they demonstrate a familiarity with at least the theoretical literature of one or more of the European languages. No equivalent expectation concerning *range in cultural literacy* is currently directed at those who work mainly, say, in French or German. At the very least, we can say that the time has now come to attend to these hierarchies as a fundamental issue to be encountered in the classroom today and in the student's preparation for a professional career in the discipline. I am speaking here not of the kinds of research projects future scholars in the field will or ought to work on, which in no way can be prejudged or predicted, but rather the kinds of literacy we hope they can *bring* to the formulation of their research. It does not seem an exaggeration or unfair to say that at least some forms of multiculturalism in the humanities today, while they claim to take their cue from Said's radical critique of the Eurocentrism of the humanities, represent an accommodation with the status quo rather than an attempt to interrogate it rigorously.

Said's most influential contribution to these debates is of course the concept and metaphor—evocative, dense, and elusive at the same time—of contrapuntality, first employed in 1984 in the essay "Reflections on Exile," but finding its fullest elaboration in *Culture and Imperialism.* The full import of this idea, the range and depth of meanings it contains, and the concrete forms it might take in reading (and teaching) practices remain as of yet largely unexplored.[8] At least implicit in Said's formulation is the possibility of fundamental transformations in the ways in which we read literature and culture. It enacts a complex relationship with the notion of tradition—linguistic, national, civilizational—that it both takes seriously and puts into question by opening up any particular tradition to interaction with other such purportedly discrete entities. This opening up and crossing over appear in Said's work as utterly historical operations that at the same time transgress the categories of traditional historicism. Thus the *Description de l'Egypte* may be viewed not just alongside al-Jabarti's contemporary account of the French in Egypt but also George Antonius's analysis of the Arab political and cultural "awakening" a century later; *Mansfield Park* may

---

8. The legion of courses that offer Brontë alongside Rhys, Conrad alongside Salih, Shakespeare with Césaire, and so on represent only an initial and very partial attempt to put this idea into pedagogical practice.

be opened up to an understanding of Eric Williams and C. L. R. James; and Conrad may be revisited with a comprehension of Tayeb Salih in hand. But, at its most expansive, contrapuntality is an argument about the nature of culture in the modern era. Through it, we come to see all ideas of cultural autonomy and autochthony as phantasmic in nature. We come to understand that societies on either side of the imperial divide now live deeply imbricated lives that cannot be understood without reference to each other. It begins to encode a comparativism yet to come, a global comparativism that is a determinate and concrete response to the hierarchical systems that have dominated cultural life since the colonial era. What is striking here is that Said saw that this disciplinary revisionism involves in part a return to the past, viewing it as a *radical renewal* of the long since lost humanistic "mission" of the early notion of world literature as a comparative terrain for the mutual interaction of the world's numerous literatures, while understanding that "the field [had been] epistemologically organized as a sort of hierarchy, with Europe and its Latin Christian literatures at its center and top," which "assume[ed] the silence, willing or otherwise, of the non-European world." For its nineteenth- and early twentieth-century proponents, the comparative study of the world's literatures was to "furnish a transnational, even trans-human perspective on literary performance."[9] This mission of comparative literary studies needed now to be reformulated and radically renewed in tune with the global demand for social justice and emancipation in the twentieth century.

Said's most extended engagement with the epistemological issues that are at stake in attending to this hierarchical structure takes form in *Orientalism*, which opened up like no other single text in the twentieth century the question of the colonial origins and Eurocentric nature of knowledge and representation in the humanistic terrain. The difficult and in many ways elusive perception that Said makes possible here is that the non-Western text is no longer available to us, is no longer readable except through the Orientalist canon in which it already comes constituted as object. No attempt at a strong encounter with the non-European text, including and especially the "classical," "precolonial," or "premodern" textuality of these traditions, can hope to bypass the Western corpus, the Orientalist system, and the terms of Western literariness itself. Said begins in *Orientalism* to develop a way of thinking about the status of non-Western culture within the production of humanistic knowledge in the West, a ground-clearing that is a necessary condition for, and a moment within,

9. Edward W. Said, *Culture and Imperialism* (New York, 1993), pp. 47, 45, 50, 45.

any attempt to reconstellate the terms of our approach to these other cultures and literatures.

There is a powerful moment in Salih's novel *Season of Migration to the North* that condenses into a single image this contemporary situation of global postcolonial culture.[10] The novel is, famously, an inversion of the narrative movements (in time as in space) of *Heart of Darkness*.[11] The Kurtz figure, as it were, appears in the person of Mustafa Sa'eed, who journeys from colonial Sudan to 1950s London, reversing the direction of the journey into the heart of darkness. Mustafa reverses the originary and ongoing violence of colonial occupation through sexual conquest, claiming to liberate Africa with his penis, seducing and ultimately driving to suicide a long series of English women precisely by manipulating, intensifying, and finally shattering their Orientalist fantasies about him as an Arab and African. He confirms their desire to see him and his world as the very antithesis of their own, as the purest expression of the barbarous, of animality, and of nature itself. Convicted finally for the murder of his English wife—who had turned the sexual tables on him and had managed, as he puts it, to convert him from hunter to quarry—Mustafa Sa'eed serves his prison term and returns to the Sudan, settling down in a remote village along the banks of the Nile, where the narrator—a native of the village who himself has just returned from England with a Ph.D. in English poetry—encounters him for the first time.

Towards the end of the novel, after he has gradually revealed to the narrator this past, entirely unknown to the peasant folk among whom he has chosen to live, Mustafa Sa'eed disappears, presumed to have drowned in the seasonal floodwaters of the Nile, and Salih leads us to believe that perhaps he had died answering the siren call of the West, of illicit desire, of conquest and sexuality. In the wake of the devastating event of his second wife's bizarre and terrifying death—she, a local village girl, forced after Mustafa's death to remarry against her will an old man in the village, kills both him and herself when he tries to consummate their marriage—the narrator returns to the village and enters a room in Mustafa Sa'eed's house that has always been kept locked and sealed from the outside world. It is the jarring juxtapositions of what he discovers in this room, in this mud house, in this village on the banks of the river Nile in the heart of Africa, that is of interest

---

10. I am using the following editions here: Al-Tayyib Salih, *Mawsim al-hijra 'ila al-shamal* (Cairo, 1969), and Tayeb Salih, *Season of Migration to the North*, trans. Denys Johnson-Davies (London, 1985). I have altered the Johnson-Davies translation as I felt necessary.

11. See Said, *Culture and Imperialism*, p. 311, and Saree Makdisi, "The Empire Renarrated: *Season of Migration to the North* and the Reinvention of the Present," *Critical Inquiry* 18 (Summer 1992): 804–20.

to me here. The room is a perfect replica of an English study and sitting room, down to the last architectural detail, down to the last object it contains, from the paintings and tapestries on the walls, to the furniture, carpets, mementos, and, last but not least, books, which are everywhere in the room:

> The books—I could see in the light of the lamp that they were arranged in categories. Books on economics, history and literature. Zoology. Geology. Mathematics. Astronomy. The Encyclopaedia Britannica. Gibbon. Macaulay. Toynbee. The complete works of Bernard Shaw. Keynes. Tawney. Smith. Robinson. *The Economics of Imperfect Competition.* Hobson, *Imperialism.* Robinson, *An Essay on Marxian Economics.* Sociology. Anthropology. Psychology. Thomas Hardy. Thomas Mann. E. G. Moore. Thomas Moore. Virginia Woolf. Wittgenstein. Einstein. Brierly. Namier. Books I had heard of and others of which I had not. Volumes of poetry by poets of whom I did not know the existence. *The Journals of Gordon. Gulliver's Travels.* Kipling. Housman. *The History of the French Revolution,* Thomas Carlyle. *Lectures on the French Revolution,* Lord Acton. Books bound in leather. Books in paper covers. Old tattered books. Books that looked as if they'd just come straight from the printers. Huge volumes the size of tombstones. Small books with gilt edges the size of packs of playing cards. Signatures. Dedications. Books in boxes. Books on the chairs. Books on the floor. What play-acting is this? What does he mean? Owen. Ford Maddox Ford. Stefan Zweig. E. G. Browne. Laski. Hazlitt. *Alice in Wonderland.* Richards. *The Qur'an* in English. *The Bible* in English. Gilbert Murray. Plato. *The Economics of Colonialism,* Mustafa Sa'eed. *Colonialism and Monopoly,* Mustafa Sa'eed. *The Cross and Gunpowder,* Mustafa Sa'eed. *The Rape of Africa,* Mustafa Sa'eed. *Prospero and Caliban. Totem and Taboo.* Doughty. Not a single Arabic book. A graveyard. A mausoleum. An insane idea. A prison. A huge joke. A treasure chamber.[12]

What Salih attempts to represent here is the immense library that is the humanistic culture of the modern West and the fate within it, specifically, of those forms of cultural otherness that come marked with the non-Western or non-European origins of the languages in which they are produced. The passage stages the global dominance of this culture, which seems here to include not only the corpus of bourgeois literature and culture but also the Western radical tradition of critique of Western society—"Robinson,

---

12. Salih, *Mawsim al-hijra 'ila al-shamal,* pp. 113–14; Salih, *Season of Migration to the North,* pp. 136–38.

An Essay on Marxian Economics"—as well as the specifically Third Worldist, radical, and internationalist critique of colonialism—"*The Cross and Gunpowder,* Mustafa Sa'eed." Above all, what this remarkable passage points to is a generalized condition of culture in the contemporary world. We see now the enormity of the problem: the non-Western text is available to us only within this immense library—"in English," in Salih's words, that is, *in translation,* assigned its place as Oriental text-object within the architecture of the Western library.

The passage stages a confrontation with the situation of the modern Arabic writer; it raises the possibility that the book in which we encounter it will itself inevitably find its ("translated" and assigned) place in this library, so the act of writing would have to be a struggle to produce a text that is not merely a dead letter, an epitaph, as it were, words carved on a tombstone. In the final pages of the novel, the narrator, having escaped from the madness of Mustafa Sa'eed's library, enters the Nile in a state of semiawareness, and nearly drowns midstream. In the last lines he comes back to consciousness of himself and his surroundings and decides to fight physically to stay alive. The end of the novel thus offers an allegorical rendering of this struggle to achieve what Abdallah Laroui once called, with respect to postcolonial Arab culture, an "adequate" literary form. In fact, the emergence in the novel of the consciousness that is the narrator parallels the emergence and modalities of what Laroui, in his classic work *L'Idéologie arabe contemporaine,* published the year following Salih's novel, described as the "double critical consciousness" necessary for a comprehension of the postcolonial situation of Arab societies, directed both at the various ideological positions in the Arab world as well as at the cultural complex that is the modern West. No self-described attempt to "return" to tradition, religious or secular, can sustain its claim to be autonomous of "the West," Laroui writes, not even that of "the religious scholar" (*clerc*) whose claim to authenticity is based on a return to the purportedly uncontaminated doxa of religious tradition: "In contemporary Arab ideology, no form of consciousness is authentic: no more so in the religious scholar than in the technophile; he reflects a different image of contact with the West, but the center of his thought is no more his own than that of the technophile belongs properly to him."[13] No attempt to explore one's *own* tradition can therefore bypass a historical critique of the West and its emergence into this particular position of dominance. In this sense, the critique of the West is in fact a *self*-critique. This is the enormous task that *Orientalism* undertakes, an attempt, as Said puts it, to "inventory the traces upon me, the Oriental subject, of the culture whose domination has been so powerful a factor in the life of all Orientals."[14] From

13. Abdallah Laroui, *L'Idéologie arabe contemporaine: Essai critique* (Paris, 1967), p. 68.
14. Said, *Orientalism* (1978; New York, 1994), p. 25; hereafter abbreviated *O.*

our present perspective, then, Edward Said's *Orientalism* may be read as an attempt to understand the architecture of Mustafa Sa'eed's library, the library that one owns and by which one is owned in turn. In the original—that is, from the perspective of modern literary Arabic—it is of course this catalogue of *English* (and more broadly European) names that appear as estranged and foreign, requiring translation, with the Qur'an—made to stand in here for the entire Arabic-Islamic tradition—undergoing a double estrangement, a double translation. The *hijra 'ila al-shamal* ("migration to the north") invoked in Salih's novel parallels what is glossed in Said's work by "the voyage in," the emergence of an oppositional consciousness that is neither fully inside nor entirely outside metropolitan, Western culture, a critical consciousness that will undertake a radical critique of Western culture as a condition for exploring "contemporary alternatives to Orientalism, to ask how one can study other cultures and peoples from a libertarian, or a nonrepressive and nonmanipulative, perspective" (*O*, p. 24).

The scope and ambition of modern Orientalism for Said is, as he famously put it, "worldly." By this he means first of all that this vast agglomeration of texts, institutions, and practices is of and in the world, participating in, and dependent upon such "projects" as the Napoleonic invasion of Egypt, the colonial life of such institutions as the Royal Asiatic Society, the building of the Suez Canal, the partitioning of the Middle East following World War I, the Palestinian catastrophe of 1948, and the further displacement and military occupation since 1967. But what Said further means by this is that the system he calls Orientalism seeks to encompass nothing less than the world itself. What is at stake, in other words, is not simply "representations" (of X, Y, or Z), as so many readers of the book have assumed, but the very nature and identity of human collectivities and the places they inhabit in the world. Hence the disconcerting, defamiliarizing intent of the statement with which *Orientalism* opens: "The Orient was almost a European invention" (*O*, p. 1). *Almost*, we might note, but not *exactly*. The assertion that "there were—and are—cultures and nations whose location is in the East" (*O*, p. 5) sounds like the awkward apologia of "discourse analysis" if we fail to recognize the tense balancing act it seeks to achieve: to assert the immense efficacy of Orientalist description over these societies while insisting at the same time that no system is so powerful as to conquer and exhaust, and thus *invent*, its human objects entirely. On the other hand, the attempt to reclaim traditions whose social basis is seen to have been destroyed by the processes of capitalist-colonial modernization, an attempt shared by numerous and varied cultural and political projects across the non-Western world today, cannot simply bypass "Orientalism"—the organizing, refractive, globally ambitious, and, in the sense that Said has made us understand, inventive culture of the modern West.

Such reclamation reverts to Orientalism more surely the more it denies the necessity of this mediation. The struggle to achieve nonrepressive and egalitarian forms of knowledge in this context takes the form of an effort at a double translation: the goal is to *invent* a language into which to translate practices that come to us *already* translated as texts-objects, a "global *translatio*," as Emily Apter has recently put it, so powerfully, but one that is keenly aware of the *already translated nature* of the objects it seeks to approach.[15] As Said repeatedly suggested, often to the confusion of some who considered themselves his political and intellectual disciples, this difficult effort would involve in part a return to, and radical revision of, possibilities inherent in the historical forms of the humanities.[16] The very *point* of his radical critique of humanistic culture is to make it adequate to the imagining of a postimperial world.

The methodological and theoretical effort that will be required of the literary discipline as a whole if it is to respond adequately to this Saidian challenge will leave no aspect of disciplinary practice unchanged, a prospect that produces at this stage of the game not only outright opposition and resentment, as it once did, but also modes of accommodation under multiculturalist, ethnic, minority, and postcolonial rubrics whose purpose, we need to admit, is to avert the possibility of that fundamental rethinking and the sense of disciplinary vertigo it produces. Above all, a critique of the modalities of Eurocentrism in our disciplines must consider the contemporary state of what I have called theory culture, whose rise and transformation remained one of the preoccupations of Said's work at least from *Beginnings* onward. Said's repeated admonishments about the fate of institutionalized theoretical speculation—the neutralization of theory's original, insurrectionary, and revolutionary affiliations and its descent into closed systems and guilds—are infused with serious doubts about its ability to question rigorously the notion of a self-contained Western tradition. I don't wish to engage in breezy generalizations about the state of the field of theory today, which in any case is not internally homogeneous, but will instead offer some observations about an influential recent work, Michael Hardt and Antonio Negri's *Empire,* in order to outline what I take to be symptomatic about its playing out of the question of Europe for contemporary global culture. The central thesis of this sweeping and immensely imaginative book, which has already become a classic of sorts within po-

15. See Emily Apter, "Global *Translatio:* The 'Invention' of Comparative Literature, Istanbul, 1933," *Critical Inquiry* 29 (Winter 2003): 253–81.

16. This point could be made at much greater length with reference to his posthumously published work, *Humanism and Democratic Criticism* (New York, 2004), an exercise that I must postpone for another occasion.

litical and cultural theory, concerns the emergence of a single, globally extensive form of sovereignty, which they call Empire in order to distinguish it from the imperialism of the preceding era. What is remarkable about the study from our perspective, however, is that this supposedly global experience of governance—of individuals, bodies, collectivities—is derived entirely and exclusively from the categories of the Western political-theoretical tradition, conceived as a self-enclosed and continuous entity. I quote a key early passage:

> The genealogy we follow in our analysis of the passage from imperialism to Empire will be first European and then Euro-American, not because we believe that these regions are the exclusive or privileged source of new ideas and historical innovation, but simply because this was the dominant geographical path along which the concepts and practices that animate today's Empire developed—in step, as we will argue, with the development of the capitalist mode of production. Whereas the genealogy of Empire is in this sense Eurocentric, however, its present powers are not limited to any region. Logics of rule that in some sense originated in Europe and the United States now invest practices of domination throughout the globe.[17]

Made in Europe, which is one of the most complex and overdetermined signifiers of the modern era, marking, to borrow from Said, "the *strength of Western cultural discourse*" in an imperialized world and the "formidable structure of cultural domination" it exercises, is deployed here with not much more self-consciousness than by those nineteenth-century commentators who speculated about the possibilities of bringing the natives into the purview of (European) civilization (*O,* p. 25). And this once and for all and total victory of Europe is established by Hardt and Negri by downscaling their usually high Deleuzian language to a fairly orthodox Marxist analysis, as in the following passage:

> There is at the base of the modern theory of sovereignty, however, a further very important element—a content that fills and sustains the form of sovereign authority. This content is represented by capitalist development and the affirmation of the market as the foundation of the values of social reproduction. Without this content, which is always implicit, always working inside the transcendental apparatus, the form of sovereignty would not have been able to survive in modernity, and European modernity would not have been able to achieve a hegemonic position on

17. Michael Hardt and Antonio Negri, *Empire* (Cambridge, Mass., 2000), pp. xv–xvi.

a world scale. As Arif Dirlik has noted, Eurocentrism distinguished itself from other ethnocentrisms (such as Sinocentrism) and rose to global prominence principally because it was supported by the powers of capital.[18]

First of all, the reliance on the remark by Arif Dirlik here is a decisive one and marks a failure to understand its full context and resonance, which is the particular trajectory of secularism and ideologies of modernization (and Europeanization) in Turkish political and intellectual life since the late Ottoman period, a history of East-West confrontation that is well known. A remark that should be read as emerging from *within* the history of Western expansion and domination and the various and varying responses of the non-European societies affected by that process is used instead to establish the *end* of the self-other dialectic inherent to it. Furthermore, and more importantly, the notion of the universalism of the logic of "capitalist development," accompanied with what appears to be at least an implicit notion that the diverse regions and societies of the world constitute the undifferentiated *field* for the elaboration of this universalist logic, is made to do the elaborate work of both sustaining the hierarchies we call Eurocentrism—"first in Europe, then elsewhere"—and making them disappear from view altogether. If such a structure of thought is implicit in numerous critiques of imperialism-as-capitalism since Lenin's great essay on the subject, it becomes acutely visible in *Empire*. It is striking, and far from insignificant, that Hardt and Negri's analysis of Empire entirely bypasses the long tradition, painstakingly elaborated in the course of the twentieth century, and stretching, say, from Gandhi and DuBois in its first decade to Said and his contemporaries in its final ones, of the critique of empire from perspectives made possible by the experience of imperial subjugation, a critical and *theoretical* tradition, surely, but one which can have only "symptomatic" value for Hardt and Negri's analysis.[19] The so-called *cultural* emphasis in Said's understanding of imperialism is a rejection of such a structure of thought and not simply an "idealist" failure to comprehend the determining impact of material and economic forces, as some of his detractors on the Left have mistakenly held. The genuine alternative to this universalism of contemporary Eurocentric thought is not a retreat into the local, into so many localities, but rather a *general* account of the play of the particular in the universalizing processes of capitalist-imperial modernity. Hardt and Negri's concept of the multitude as a global oppositional force within Empire is at one level a thoroughgoing revision of the concept of class in Marxist analysis. But if the authors took at all seriously theoretical work that is

18. Ibid., pp. 85–86.
19. See ibid., pp. 137–59.

not comfortably aligned within the Western tradition they might have found useful, for instance, the collective work in Indian historiography known as subaltern studies, which has undertaken a significant rethinking of the concept of class in its elaboration of the concept of the subaltern, precisely in terms of the question of capital's encounter with alterity in the colonies.

In its moments of emergence, contemporary "theory" is clearly animated by an anti-imperialist impulse, both in general and in relation to particular contexts of imperial violence and liberationist struggle—the French imbroglio in Algeria with regard to figures like Sartre, Barthes, Foucault, and Derrida, and opposition to the American war in Indochina in the context of the American appropriation or reigniting of these figures and their work. (And Hardt and Negri's credentials in this regard are certainly unimpeachable.) My concern here is not with anti-imperialism per se as a political position or viewpoint but rather with the ways in which theory has come to be constituted today as a knowledge field at least in the Anglo-American academy, and Hardt and Negri's work is useful for me here for the ways in which it performs the limits of the field. The kinds of observations I have made here about this significant work are not the ones that would naturally arise in theory contexts as they are presently constituted. In the aftermath of the great multiculturalist onslaught in the U.S. over the last two decades—the demand for inclusive curricula, revisionist and "contrapuntal" readings of the Western literary canon, and the emergence of new, relatively privileged (if ghettoized) fields of literary study—one cannot help suspecting that the culture of theory has become a last defense and redoubt for some of its inhabitants, a place of safety and refuge from the imperatives of what Said calls contrapuntality; it can be granted that "they" have literatures and other modes of cultural expression that are worthy of consideration, but only "we" have theory, the inclination to think in abstract and conceptual terms about language, culture, and the world and about the conditions of possibility of such knowledge itself. There are of course notable counterexamples to this posture—Susan Buck-Morss's highly original and commendable recent attempt at putting Western political theory in conversation with the Islamist thought of the modern era, Judith Butler's philosophical and historical critique of the psychology of militarism and war in the present moment, Ackbar Abbas's displacement and revision of Benjaminian motifs from Paris and Berlin to Hong Kong, and Ronald Judy's fascinating engagements with Salafist philosophy, to name but three contemporary instances—but I have no hesitation in saying that these are exceptions to the rule.[20]

20. See Susan Buck-Morss, *Thinking Past Terror: Islamism and Critical Theory on the Left* (London, 2003); Judith Butler, *Precarious Life: The Powers of Mourning and Violence* (London,

In an article about the possibility of reviving a conception of world literature for our own era, Franco Moretti has argued that there is no other reason "for the existence of departments of comparative literature" than "to be a thorn in the side, a permanent intellectual challenge to national literatures."[21] This is a salutary reminder, but we may add that the biggest question facing comparative literary studies as an intellectual formation today, in which the very contours of the discipline are at stake, is whether it can produce an adequate disciplinary response to the challenge that it attempt to become a *planetary* discipline, that is, that it attempt to undo or at least seriously examine the linguistic and literary hierarchies that are its foundation. Here Moretti ultimately fails to provide direction, the systematizing impulse and "distant reading" problematic he proposes preempting the possibility of disciplinary refashioning of the sort I have proposed here and which is one direction in which Said's work in literary studies may now be taken. In terms of institutional location, much of the innovative work of the last quarter century for which comparatists can rightly take credit is now possible to pursue in the national departments, under such rubrics as Anglophone or Francophone literature, global Englishes, literature of the Americas, and so on. The contribution that departments of comparative literature can make at this stage, it seems to me, concerns non-Western languages and literatures in particular, the nature of their marginalization by the rise and global dominance of the Western European languages, and how and whether they may be taught and studied on an equal footing. This will mean not just adding literatures to the curriculum that have not been taught before in comparative literature departments but rethinking how the "core" literatures and theoretical traditions themselves may be taught within a disciplinary framework of global comparativism. There is at this point no other overall raison d'etre that is original and *specific* to comparative literature as an institutional location. Admittedly, this is a very large, ambitious, even vertiginous charge, but in order to take it seriously we can attend to some very concrete questions, in particular the ways in which language and literary field requirements for the graduate degree as they presently exist structure the discipline. The ACLA's decade-old suggestion that we encourage students to acquire non-European languages must now be renewed and given the force of something more than a suggestion. In order to displace and realign the axis of "comparison" for our discipline from *Europe*

2004); and Ronald Judy, "Sayyid Qutb's *fiqh al-waqi'i* or New Realist Science," *Boundary 2* 31 (Summer 2004): 113–48.

21. Franco Moretti, "Conjectures on World Literature," *New Left Review*, no. 1 (Jan.–Feb. 2000): 68.

or the West to *the planet,* we will have to require a different kind of cultural and intellectual range than we traditionally have.

Meaningful comparative training today has to include the acquisition of skills and thought habits that facilitate this move and make possible a concrete understanding of such global polarities as North and South, East and West, and the ways in which they continue to structure the very possibilities of knowledge in our field. To act as if we do not distinguish between the world's languages and simply allow any student to study, say, Hindi, Kikuyu, or Chinese to fulfill the degree requirements does not, as I have already noted, change the nature of what constitutes the core of the discipline. In my view, the time has now come to discuss the possibility of requiring of all our students at least some familiarity with a non-European language and a cultural context—be it literary or otherwise artistic, philosophical, or critical—whose knowledge is facilitated by that linguistic ability. What exactly non-European or non-Western means in this context is, as I have already argued, a question open to multiple and contingent solutions, historically interpretable, and certainly not reducible to continental or civilizational terms. What should be stressed, I think, is distance and *range*—historical, morphological, cultural—and a sense of the need to attend to those numerous, varied languages and literary traditions, written as well as oral, that have become marginalized and subalternized upon entering into the global literary and cultural systems since the colonial era. I can envision, for instance, students whose primary research language is French being also interested in studying Arabic or Vietnamese, while those who are Germanists studying, say, Turkish, and Latin Americanists working in Spanish or Portuguese also acquiring knowledge of a native, pre-Columbian language and cultural context.[22] But under certain circumstances someone in French, German, or Italian studies might look to, say, Polish, Russian, Greek, or Serbo-Croatian in order to achieve this range. Under others, Irish may be considered as the first historically to suffer the fate of non-Western languages. On the other hand, students whose primary formation or abilities are in non-Western languages should be required to have more than a passing familiarity with the imaginative or theoretical literatures of at least one of the languages that have historically constituted the core of the discipline. None of this will be easy to do, and different institutions will have to formulate such new requirements in terms of their own particular strengths and needs. The assumption that the inclusion of literatures that have not been part of comparative literature's purview will require a watering down of the language requirements, however, is a spurious one. If anything, they

22. For this last suggestion, I am grateful to my colleague Efrain Kristal.

will have to be made more complex—distinguishing, for instance, between the different kinds of linguistic formation that students bring to graduate study and between their main research languages and the secondary languages that are meant to expand their cultural literacy—and in some ways more difficult for students to fulfill.

As I have tried to show, Said demonstrated a quarter century ago that "nonrepressive and nonmanipulative" forms of knowledge in the future in the humanities would have to be more encompassing and more comparatist, not less, than scholarship has been in the recent past. My concern here has been with the disciplinary conditions in comparative literary studies that appear to me to be obstacles to its emergence. Whether or not the kind of restructuring I have proposed in these final comments would lead ultimately to the results imagined by Said is of necessity an open question. Regardless, it seems an interesting and exciting thing to discuss, to explore, and to attempt. In doing so, we would be expressing a desire to pick up where he left off in *Orientalism* a quarter century ago. This would be a fitting repayment of the debt he has left those of us who live and work in the humanities.

Conversation with Edward Said

Roger Owen

Dear Edward,

I am writing to you while looking at the photograph Sulayman Khalaf took of us sitting on a bench at the University of Mainz during the WOC-MES conference in 2002. We are obviously in the middle of a conversation, but it's difficult to tell who is talking.

One thing the photograph brings to mind is that, although we always took great pleasure in our, often accidental, meetings we were probably discussing personal matters interspersed with a certain amount of academic gossip. It was as though our rare conversations were too precious to spoil with reference either to that week's news from the Middle East—reactions to which I think we always assumed we shared—or to our thoughts about what each was then writing or had just written.

Now, however, when it is no longer possible to enjoy the pleasure of your company, I would love to be able to address some of the questions that we always seem to have avoided, beginning with our different approaches to what, even in the early 1970s, was starting to be called Orientalism. This was a method of analyzing the Middle East, its peoples and its history, to which I and the British-based members of what was to be called the Hull group had begun to critique in conferences and in our *Review of Middle East Studies,* which first came out in 1975. Part of our purpose was to expose some of its basic preconceptions, particularly as they related to the use made of its authority to support certain colonialist, imperialist, and Zionist enterprises. Part was to examine how such politically charged obscurantism might be replaced as a method of understanding the Middle East by a set of tools and techniques drawn from a universalist reading of the social sciences, particularly anthropology, sociology, and political economy.

I remember very well my initial excitement at reading the draft text of *Orientalism* you sent me and the clear impression that you had done such a good job at undermining the authority of the old guard that the first part of our own work of critique could now be laid aside for the more constructive task of finding better ways to study the Middle East. But I soon became aware that several of my colleagues were less sanguine than I, arguing that, in some ways, your book had made our task more difficult by the way it appeared to undercut the possibility of a universalist approach to the analysis of Eastern societies, however much we might laud the universal humanism of your project.

Looking back on it now I see that one of the reasons for the difference between me and my colleagues was that I was one of the very few who taught in a Middle East center and so was in day-to-day battle with all the shocking misrepresentations, distortions, and belittlements of the region and its peoples to be found in so many of the standard texts. If I understand your own first encounter with the Orientalist literature correctly, this was something you and I both shared? But it did raise questions that I would have very much liked to discuss with you both then and now.

Roger

Dear Roger,

Thank you for your letter. I too have enjoyed our conversations and recognized our shared sense of reticence when it came to avoidance of potentially divisive subjects. More importantly, I have also believed in a kind of division of labor in which we both tried to do what we did best, something that I indicated in a number of short passages in *Orientalism* when I pointed to you as one of those who believed the study of man and society is best conducted within the broad field of all the social sciences.

You will remember my telling you at our first meeting in Oxford after its publication that I had grown tired during the writing of chapter three in Palo Alto and was anxious to finish the manuscript as quickly as possible. This had the great advantage to me, personally, of not having to plow through so much of the depressing work of the mid-twentieth-century Orientalists. It may also have liberated me from having to cover so large a field, allowing me to concentrate on those areas where my notion of Orientalism could best be used as a basis for exploring important issues of cul-

Roger Owen teaches Middle East history at Harvard University. He is the author of several works on Middle East political and economic history as well as, most recently, *Lord Cromer: Victorian Imperialist, Edwardian Proconsul* (2004).

ture and imperialism along the lines of a research agenda first suggested in the introduction to my book.

Nevertheless, it was soon clear that some of these initial notions had to be revised. It is true that, for awhile, the interest in my book, and then in *Culture and Imperialism,* shown by scholars in feminist, postcolonial, architectural, and other studies, took me away from a direct academic concern for the Middle East. But I was soon drawn back for a number of personal, political, and intellectual reasons. Like you, I probably started off with what proved to be an overly optimistic belief that once we had managed to remove the "mind-forg'd manacles" of teachers and students of the Middle East, both Middle Eastern and foreign, they would immediately be free to view the region in a more nuanced, more historically truthful way. But this was to ignore at least two important problems. One was the fact that *Orientalism* was immediately seized upon by some of its detractors as a political text containing a dangerous, if covert, agenda that they felt the need to contest. The other was that the work of guiding students through the canonical Orientalist works of Middle Eastern history, religion, and culture seems to have proved more difficult than I had initially imagined, given the fact that, whatever their faults, these works remained a major repository of knowledge about the region.

Second, what neither you nor I could have anticipated was the impact of Islamic revolution in Iran, the study of which demanded an understanding of political religion that none of us had ever imagined we would want to possess. This at once provided a space for those who professed such an expertise to recover some of their lost authority, as well as, more importantly, to remake the argument that religion was the key to understanding not just the politics of the Middle East but also its alleged economic and social backwardness.

The effect was certainly to personalize and politicize the impact of my book, at least as far as the study of the Middle East was concerned. This may or may not have been made worse by the way *Orientalism* was itself used year after year in many courses aimed at introducing students to the region, not as an essay in the association between a certain kind of power and knowledge but as an example either of a sort of litmus test of correctness or, worse still, of one of the many kinds of *isms* ("Said-ism") that all aspiring graduates should be able to identify, discuss, and then file away for future reference.

How this affected your own academic work I'm not sure. For my part, as I assert in the preface to the twenty-fifth anniversary edition of *Orientalism,* although "I have never taught *anything* about the Middle East," it certainly involved me in a number of debates on a number of different fronts about the implication of the notion of Orientalism for Middle Eastern studies including its use to authorize the misrepresentation of regional realities both inside the universities and without. As a result I was forced to define my own position about the contemporary Middle East more precisely, not just about the struggle for Palestine, in which I was becoming ever more closely involved, but also about such central questions as the nature of Arab government, the shortcomings in Arab education, and the role of censorship in limiting free expression.

Where does this leave us now? Well, for one thing, we are united in a battle with a contemporary Orientalism that is proving to be a much more resilient creature than we once supposed. For another, it is clear that its critique cannot proceed without paying some attention to the realities that it aims to hide, mystify, or distort. Hence we need a different division of labor than the one I originally envisaged, based, perhaps, on different notions of what it is to try to "understand" the Middle East, I through the lens of humanism and world history, you via the tools of political and socioeconomic analysis, international comparison, and, where possible, the testimony of the important actors concerned.

Edward

Dear Edward,

Your helpful reply suggests a number of related topics on which I would very much like your opinion. One concerns your views on the relationship between the academic and the political. While I fully share your notion of the role of the engaged intellectual I am anxious to know more about your own experience of how and where to draw the line between the two. My own mentor in this matter was Albert Hourani, who imagined a kind of geographical distance between the two, with Oxford representing the one and London the other. More recently I have imagined something of the same distinction between what I write and teach in and around the university and the articles I write for *Al-Hayat* and elsewhere.

But both you and I know that it's more complicated than that and that much of the authority behind the political writings of academics about the Middle East comes from their own standing as scholars, even if this is generally easier to see in the works of those with whom we disagree than those we write ourselves. There is a kind of necessary disingenuousness about this by which politically engaged scholars have to claim a status for their academic work on the Middle East that it doesn't quite possess, even to the point of cultivating a kind of innocent outrage at the notion that what they profess academically could be seen in more than one light. Perhaps this is part of the price we have to pay to maintain our own intellectual independence, of showing that we are not at the service of anyone else's political agenda?

What may also complicate the issue is that those of us who speak and write publicly about the Middle East must always have two audiences in mind—the Western (American and European) and the Middle Eastern—and that the business of trying to explain one to the other also involves strategies and choices of a political nature. It is good to assert as you do in *The End of the Peace Process* that we have a duty to "let the facts (about what is going on in Palestine) speak for themselves." Nevertheless, we both know that there is a good deal more to it than that. I'm also aware that we both have personal agendas for the peoples of the Middle East that go beyond your obviously political late-1990s reminder that Palestinians should be aware that it was still possible to reverse the Oslo peace process—for example, your call for the Arabs to learn more about the United States or my insistence that they can only begin to understand their own modern history when they have before them a series of good biographies of their own leaders, from Nasser onwards.

Roger

Dear Roger,

I know what you mean. But let me try to think it through from my own experience. As I wrote in *Out of Place* I did not become politically engaged until 1967. Before then, as I tried to explain, there was a dissociation between my life in America during a time of extreme political quiescence and in the Middle East where I was aware of, but did not directly participate in, the major trends of the time. Even after 1967 my engagement with Palestine came for many years largely through my association with the Association of Arab-American University Graduates (the AAUG), which pursued the type of politics generally associated with a professional pressure group designed to inform, to raise consciousness if you like, and to remind politicians that there was another side to the question of Palestine.

As a result, so it seems to me, it was only with the publication of *Orientalism* in 1978 that I was forced to face the question you ask about the overlap between scholarship and politics. It was a painful moment as I tried to demonstrate in my afterword to the 1994 edition. I say there that some hostile attention was to be expected. But I was unpleasantly surprised by what seemed to me the willful misrepresentation of my argument as being either anti-Western or pro-Arab, pro-Islamic. Some of this—I don't quite know how much—came from the assumption that, being identified as a Palestinian/Arab, I must be writing from that point of view.

It was also clear that one of the easiest ways to divert attention from my root-and-branch criticism both of Orientalism and the institutions that supported it was to try to undermine the book's academic credentials by implying an underlying political agenda.

Did I have such an agenda? In one sense, of course, I did. The book was certainly written against a powerful body of writing that I believed to have exerted a malign influence on the way in which Europeans and Americans regarded what they were encouraged to perceive as a different order of human beings. But I also believed that I had done so according to the best traditions of scholarship and in the interests of that process of mental emancipation which is the teacher's main goal. For the rest, the fact that I was at some remove from the day-to-day business of studying the Middle East helped to maintain my sense of scholarly independence. So too did the fact that, once my political-cum-academic opponents realized that the book was being taken seriously enough to make it impervious to ad hominem attack, they turned to its supposed academic imperfections with the intention, I would suppose, of trying to buttress their own authority before their often wavering students. Hence the importance of my repeated exchanges with Bernard Lewis, who took upon himself the role of champion of the Orientalists against someone he seemed to believe could be found guilty of the simplest schoolboy howlers.

Later on, as my involvement with Palestinian politics intensified, I still continued to see my contribution as coming first and foremost from my sense of history and from the steadiness and sense of human possibility that my long study of Vico provided. Then, the more I became aware of the tremendous weaknesses of the Arafat leadership I also began to look for, and to try to encourage, the emergence, based on my AAUG experience, of a group combining exiles and the people of the West Bank that could use its independence of mind to provide an alternative to Mr. Arafat's unprincipled line.

Trying to think about all this from your own point of view I imagine your experience as being somewhat different, beginning with membership in the Labor Party, that natural home for opponents of the British status quo, and participating directly in protests against British imperial misadventures in the Middle East from Cyprus and Suez onwards? And then sequentially as a student and a teacher of Middle Eastern studies, combining this with an outsider's support for Nasserism and Arab nationalism so long as they seemed to provide a credible way to achieve real Arab independence? But what I think we did share was what I describe at the end of *Out of Place* as the "anti-authoritarianism" of the outsider and the wish to shatter and dispel what we felt to be "an unjust Establishment order."

Edward

Dear Edward,

My last set of questions stems from a combination of related observations about your life in the late 1990s and the early years of the twenty-first century. Apart from the physical pain, this time was obviously marked not only by the worsening situation in Palestine but also by the impact of President Bush's war on terrorism and the return of a particularly vicious form of what you have called "latent Orientalism," just when we had begun to suppose that its worst excesses were at end. Where you found the strength to cope with all this in such a steady fashion I don't know, although, as you indicated in your writings it was not a matter of some innate optimism but rather of a deep "faith" in the emancipatory project that the humanist tradition in teaching and scholarship will always continue to provide.

Somehow or other, in ways I don't understand, this seems to have also had something to do with your interest in a late style. As I heard you talk about it in your marvelous and moving Harvard lecture in April 2000, I cannot have been the only member of the audience to imagine that, in some measure, you were talking about yourself and the tension you felt between a wish for harmony (especially among different peoples) and the instinctive drive for that creative disharmony, of rebelliousness rather than resignation, which ensures that intellectual struggle is never done and that scholars and others will be unable, ever, to lay the ideas of such a person to rest. If the usual frustrating last-minute technical hitch had not prevented you from playing us your chosen examples from Beethoven's last quartets we might perhaps have learned just how such an act of endless self-regeneration might be performed. As it is I have to read all this into your own last articles and essays where you often seem to be tilting at the windmills of human incomprehensibility.

Autobiography may provide some help here. I would very much like your response to my own strongly held conviction that, by the end of the twentieth century, when almost all of the ideologies that had sustained us appear to have been so comprehensively discredited, our own personal stories of how we negotiated these sometimes heady, always troubled and difficult, often dangerous decades while keeping some kind of balance and human perspective is all that we have left. In your own particular case, the notion of displacement and then of being out-of-place also seemed to provide something even more interesting, a position almost outside history from which to observe how all things change and how all things remain possible.

Roger

Dear Roger,

I'm not sure I know. You might say that I was looking for a way of ending and what better way than to do so than in the company of genius. You might also say that once I had read Adorno's powerful analysis of Beethoven's late style I was in the grip of a vital idea that I simply had to explore and amplify regardless. Or maybe I had found a way towards a less geographically defined out-of-placeness where sounds and words reach out and confuse and transcend themselves to find truths that, as in Lear's mad abnegation, could be found in no other way? Or perhaps all three?

But even that may not be the point. Perhaps we just need all such ideas to keep us forever on our toes, to indicate that, however compelling our desire for harmony and closure, there can never be such a thing as the last word.

Edward

Edward Said in Bombay

Gyan Prakash

"But Gyan, what will I say? I am not an urban sociologist," Edward Said wrote me in an email.

It was 2003, and he was responding to my invitation to deliver a lecture in the Urban Reflections lecture series that I had instituted in the Cities: Society, Space, and History program of the Shelby Cullom Davis Center for Historical Studies at Princeton University. I had started this lecture series because I wanted to invite prominent intellectuals, including those who were not scholars of the city, to reflect on urban questions in a historical perspective. What did they think of the city as society? What had the promises of urbanity once been, and what were they today? What did they think of the city as a site of critical imaginations? Edward had seemed a natural for this purpose, and I was immensely pleased when he almost instantly accepted my invitation. But evidently he was having second thoughts. So I wrote back that I did not invite him as an urban sociologist nor did I want him to pretend to be one. Couldn't he draw on his memories of Cairo to reflect on the geography of the colonial cities? Or speak about his remembrance of Jerusalem in light of the Palestinian flight and Israeli domination? No, he did not want to be "memoirish." I thought about the matter and then asked if it wasn't the case that the open, democratic air promised by the modern city had been implicit in the thoughts of the anticolonial intellectuals about whom he had written so eloquently? And, in any case, hadn't they all been urban intellectuals? Couldn't he explore the place of the city in the imagination of postcolonial futures? Wasn't his concept of secular criticism related to urbanity? Edward wrote back instantly: "Suggestive as ever! Now I am excited to do the lecture, if health permits." I never thought then that the conditional clause in his sentence would actually assert its force with such finality as it did on 25 September 2003.

Edward Said's passing away left many conversations and projects unfinished, not the least of which is the struggle for an independent Palestinian homeland. But Edward was not a one-dimensional intellectual; an impressive range of intellectual undergrowth nourished even his single-minded and resolute political commitments to the cause of Palestine and to anti-imperialism. My conversation with him on the city, cut short so abruptly by his death, reflected this quality of his intellectual and political interests and their enormous range.

This conversation began in Bombay. It was November 2000, and I had been in the city for about a month, exploring the idea of writing on it. One day I happened to chance on Said's *"Reflections on Exile" and Other Essays*. My eyes leapt to the essay on the remembered Cairo of his youth.[1] It is a wonderful evocation of Cairo as a cosmopolitan city. The European influence was plentiful and dominant. The most prominent European presence was, understandably, the British Cairo, visible, among other places, in the immaculately maintained polo fields, racetrack, football fields, and bowling greens of the Gezira Club. There were, in addition, other cultural enclaves—French, Italian, Greek, Belgian, American, Jewish, and Syrian. Said writes about growing up in this Cairo of an annual opera and ballet season, recitals, concerts, tennis, golf, regular performances by the Comédie Française and the Old Vic (see "CR," pp. 272–73). It was a Cairo that was immensely malleable to European cultural influences but only fitfully open to its Arab and Islamic lives. Deeply aware of this division between the European world and Arab world, Said speaks of his fleeting encounters with native Cairenes on the street and in public places. He describes these encounters as a "contact with nature," as opposed to the highly processed, cultivated, and disciplined world he inhabited. Said evokes these brief encounters to speak about the

---

1. See Edward W. Said, "Cairo Recalled: Growing up in the Cultural Crosscurrents of 1940s Egypt," *"Reflections on Exile" and Other Essays* (Cambridge, Mass., 2000), pp. 268–75; hereafter abbreviated "CR."

GYAN PRAKASH is professor of history and director of the Shelby Cullom Davis Center for Historical Studies at Princeton University. He is the author of *Another Reason: Science and the Imagination of Modern India* (1999) and *Bonded Histories: Genealogies of Labor Servitude in Colonial India* (1990) and coauthor, with Robert L. Tignor, of *Worlds Together, Worlds Apart: A History of the Modern World from the Mongol Empire to the Present* (2002). He is the editor of *After Colonialism: Imperial Histories and Postcolonial Displacements* (1995), among other volumes.

traffic between Europe and Cairo, about a time when Cairo was "cosmopolitan, free, full of wonderful privileges" ("CR," pp. 274, 274). Then, it could be home to someone like Ignace Tiegerman, a Polish-Jewish pianist who played Chopin and Schumann with great elegance and lived an expatriate life in Cairo. For Said, the most poignant image of this Cairo was watching Tiegerman listen to an exceptionally talented student of his: she was a mother of four, a "devout Muslim," who played the piano with her head completely covered by a veil ("CR," p. 275). Understandably, this Cairene trafficking of the "ultra-European" and the "ultra-Islamic Arab" came to an end with the city's Arabization under Nasser.

It was uncanny to read Said's account in Bombay where a decidedly melancholy discourse about the decline of the cosmopolitan city was in the air. I had gone to Bombay to explore and understand the city's captivating imaginations, its representation as a place of desire and dreams, but what I encountered there was a portrait of cosmopolitan Bombay in ruins. My conversations with the city's residents, the newspaper and magazine commentaries, and literary and academic writings drew a picture of irreversible transformation. Where once textile mills and docks had hummed Bombay's siren song, there was now the cacophony of the postindustrial megalopolis. Old Bombay was no more, killed not by decay and stagnation but by choking urbanization. In place of the clearly defined city of mills, workers in the textile industry and on the docks, and trade unions, there was now the socially amorphous world of the megacity strung out slackly between its rich and poor ends. Civic services were straining at the seams under the pressure exerted by explosive and unplanned growth. Nativist passions, communal riots, the nexus between corrupt politicians and greedy businessmen had destroyed civic consciousness and wrecked the city as a coherent and cosmopolitan space. Hanging over the city was the ominous shadow cast by the Shiv Sena, the political party that had bullied its way into dominating the political landscape by using a toxic brew of nativist and communal propaganda, spiked with a generous supply of vitriolic rhetoric and muscle power. Many recalled with horror the communal fire, stoked by the Shiv Sena, that had consumed the lives of hundreds of Muslims in 1992–93 and was followed by bomb blasts that ripped through the city. The experience of violence had led several intellectuals to wonder if Bombay's cosmopolitanism had been just a facade, now as charred as the buildings incinerated in the fiery explosions. Clearly, the corpses of riot victims and the twisted metal and shattered glass of bombed office buildings were not the only debris left behind by these grim events. Political commentators inside and outside Bombay spoke with great sadness about the passing away of something equally valued—Bombay's self-image as a modern, cosmopolitan city.

Three years later, when the Shiv Sena officially renamed Bombay, calling it Mumbai, the rechristening seemed to formalize the transformation that had already occurred.

Powerful and compelling though these accounts were, I read in their melancholy representations the desire for the city as a place of promise; the longing for an optimistic urban future appeared to animate the pessimistic denouement of the present as history. Whatever else cities may be, they almost always represent an aspiration, a desire for a better future. Exploitation, domination, poverty, malnutrition, and violence may be the daily reality for many city dwellers, but cities are also spaces of hope where millions of willing and unwilling migrants seek a better life. It was this aspiration, an "optimism of the will," that was intrinsic to Said's "pessimism of the intellect." Something of this relationship between criticism and desire was what I had in mind when I wrote to him about the promise of the city implicit in the anticolonial intellectuals' imagination of postcolonial futures. To the extent that cities are places of fabricated identities and affiliations rather than filiations, to use Said's terms, urbanity is also related to his concept of secular criticism as nontheological thought. To be sure, Said's writings did not clearly articulate and develop these connections between urbanity and his critical concepts, but I did not read his evocation of cosmopolitan Cairo as mere nostalgia.

Indeed, another way of understanding the discourse about cosmopolitanism's decline is to keep in mind what Said remembers so fondly: not the "imported mythology" of European superiority, not the protocols of the colonial order, but Tiegerman and the veiled pianist, figures made possible by colonialism but also exceeding its logic of separation and segregation. Nasserite Cairo ruled out the possibility of such figures, but nonetheless Said welcomes the city's Arabization because it dismantled the controls imposed by European rule. New forms of urban encounters were opened.

A vivid sense of postcolonial Cairo's urban promise can be found in Said's essay "Cairo and Alexandria." He notes at the beginning of this essay that when he lived in Egypt he experienced the two cities as smells, sights, and sounds—"Alexandria ruled by wind and sea, Cairo by river and desert."[2] When he visited the two cities three decades later, in 1989, he saw them as historical, political, and cultural sites. He notes Egypt's transformation under Nasser and Sadat, the effects of the 1967 war, and the aftermath of Camp David. The prominent political optic of his vision renders Said a very different kind of flaneur. Unlike Walter Benjamin's gaze, Said's is captured

2. Said, "Cairo and Alexandria," *"Reflections on Exile" and Other Essays*, p. 337; hereafter abbreviated "CA."

not by the play of capital but by the effects of politics. Arabized, Cairo offers a different kind of tableau from that in which Tiegerman and the veiled pianist appeared. Now the air is more democratic. At Midan el Tahrir, the plaza at the center of the city, Said spots

> the scraggly peasant family alighting from a provincial bus; the group of young men, newspapers furled under their arms, joking together and eating *tirmus* (lupin beans in brine); a handful of elderly Effendis (office workers or government employees); an increasingly large number of *muhaggabat* (veiled women), often walking (improperly) with a young man, and likely in Cairo to have dressed up their veil with a little ornament or feather, or to set it off with a flirtatious lifting of the eyebrows. ["CA," p. 338]

Across on Gezira Island, where the Gezira Club, the fabled but faded symbol of British colonialism, stands, he notices a more democratic and varied urban scene of tennis players, swimmers, and picnickers. The city had grown from three million in 1960 to fourteen million in 1990, when Said wrote his essay; yet, he notes, one feels a sense of space. Walking and loitering are valued pleasures, and places of rest spring up unpredictably around food vendors on the streets: "Mill about there for a while (eating is not recommended unless you have built up strong immunity) and you will feel not a spectator but a participant in the life of a city bound together like the many branches of a family" ("CA," p. 339). The end of colonialism had made this Cairo possible. Now, the right to the city is not simply an assertion of entitlement to political privileges or to particular objects of consumption. Rather, it is a claim for a more expansive right to urban life or, in Henri Lefebvre's terms, to urbanity as an oeuvre, as a polyvalent and polysensorial world of work and play, isolation and encounter, similarity and difference, and symbolic and creative activities.[3]

The right to urban life in Said's postcolonial Cairo goes hand in hand with a sense of live history. Said writes about Cairo spilling beyond the colonial limits to include new districts, making it as historically rich and layered as Rome and Athens. Yet, history in Cairo has not been museumized; the past often fades away unmemorialized or, in as confusing a way as the city itself, memorialized in jarring juxtapositions rather than in a carefully arranged and preserved fashion. While Western visitors gravitate toward ancient monuments and museums, in Said's Cairo competing and conflic-

---

3. See Henri Lefebvre, *Writings on Cities*, trans. Eleonore Kofman and Elizabeth Lebas (Oxford, 1996), pp. 147–49.

tual histories coexist. The new coexists with and intrudes on the old. "Cairo fends for itself, and history must do the same" ("CA," p. 341).

Like Said's Cairo, Bombay also resists the organization of its history in a neat evolutionary fashion. Different histories live cheek by jowl, all jumbled up, resisting their representation as a smooth movement from cosmopolitanism to nativism and communalism. Exploding urbanization, the death of the textile industry and trade unions, and the rise of the Shiv Sena have transformed the city, but Bombay still represents the promise of the city as society. When I described Bombay in this fashion to Edward when I saw him after the lecture that he delivered at Princeton in 2001, he insisted that surely ethnic violence must queer my pitch. Fresh from my visit to Bombay, I enthusiastically countered by saying that just as colonial cosmopolitanism was a powerful but partial representation, so too is the image of Bombay as a city consumed by ethnic passions and conflicts. Influential though the Shiv Sena is, it operates in a city of diverse and divergent histories that existed side by side. Attracted by the city's position as the hub of manufacturing, finance, and the film industry, people from all over India have washed up on the island. They speak different languages—Marathi, Gujarati, Hindi, Urdu, Bengali, Tamil, Malayalam, and English—practice different faiths—Hinduism, Islam, Christianity, Zoroastrianism, and Jainism—and belong to different castes and classes. Historically, immigrants from villages and small towns have managed their assimilation into the modern metropolis by maintaining their native tongues and cultures in their homes and neighborhoods; Bombay's map is a jigsaw puzzle of distinct neighborhoods marked by community, language, religion, dress, and cuisine. In offices, factories, and bazaars, however, the languages of work and business in the modern city provide the means for communicating across difference. Bombayites have even concocted a hybrid but wonderfully expressive vernacular for everyday communication– Bambaiya—across linguistic borders. Western theorists and writers have often thought of the city as a space of public conversation, but Bombay literally invented a mongrel language to make communication possible among its diverse citizens. The city has long been known as a place that successfully manages the modern condition of the transitory togetherness of strangers; it has excelled in devising a makeshift and everyday art of dealing with the experience of diversity and discord. This has never evolved into a full-blown philosophy or ideology or gained the visibility of the elegant and elite ideal of cosmopolitanism, but it forms the stuff of Bombay's daily life. And even the image of the cosmopolitan city's ruins, I pointed out to Edward, expresses the ethical ideal of urbanity in the present though it disguises itself as a representation of the past.

When I spoke with Edward, I had not fully read or understood the arguments about urbanity implicit in his reminiscences and observations of Cairo, or I would have responded to his questions with insights from his own work. Instead, I relied largely on my enthusiasm and intuition. To my great benefit, I have returned to his essays to carry on the conversation with him that began in Bombay and continued episodically in person and electronically.

An important part of that conversation was my desire to get him to actually visit Bombay so he could see with his own eyes the picture I had sketched. Somehow, the city had not figured in his itinerary when he visited India in 1997. He had been to Delhi and Calcutta where a heady air of anticolonial and Third World solidarity greeted him. He had found these sentiments rejuvenating and asked me if Bombay would have been different.

I assured him that while Bombay, too, could have feted him with similar political sentiments, it would also have engaged him in an urban and urbane conversation about the predicaments and promises of living the life of difference and invention in the modern world. I said that he would have found this engagement worthy, for hadn't the desire for an open refashioning of society lain at the back of anticolonial struggles, and doesn't that still animate the aspiration today to live lives that exceed the horizon of powerful nation-states? Then I told him about Saeed Mirza, a Bombay filmmaker who directs gritty motion pictures about the city. Mirza had never met Said, but he had read him and had asked me to extend his greetings to Edward. So, I did. Edward's eyes gleamed as he said, "So, when do we go there?"

Belated Occupation, Advanced Militarization: Edward Said's Critique of the Oslo Process Revisited

Dan Rabinowitz

The late 1980s and the 1990s stand out as one of the most fateful phases in the history of the conflict over Israel/Palestine. It is also the one least properly understood. Starting in late 1987 with the intifada, the first significant Palestinian uprising against the Israeli occupation of the West Bank and Gaza Strip since 1967, it was initially shaped by the resolution of the Palestinian National Council (PNC) in Algiers (1988) to adopt a formula for a two-state solution for Israel/Palestine. Edward W. Said, who was a close adviser to Yasir Arafat at that stage, played a crucial role in bringing the PNC to make this historic leap. In many ways this resolution represents the zenith of Said's power to influence major political processes as they unfolded.

The first Gulf War and the international conference in Madrid that came in its aftermath in 1991 had Israel, under a right-wing Likud government, negotiating publicly with Jordan, Syria, Lebanon, and, indirectly, with a Palestinian delegation. This signaled the start of a decade that many still associate with hope for lasting peace but that has since become consumed by and (con)fused with the violence that has defined the region since September 2000.

Conventional wisdom in Israel and the United States suggests that the phased withdrawals of Israel, agreed to and partly executed as part of the Madrid-Oslo process between 1991 and 1999, as well as the attempts to reach a final settlement at Camp David in 2000, were steps in the right direction woefully subverted by irrational, primordial ethnic hatred and religious extremism. But anyone who was prepared to listen to Said's views of the process as it began unfolding in the 1990s had to be skeptical. A retrospective, counterfactual revisitation today of Said's comments on the Oslo process in fact renders any attempt obsolete to single out the 1990s as a decade of hope flanked by bloody remissions. What remains instead is an analysis that frames the tragic violence we see now as the inevitable result of a decade of misguided, sometimes malicious choices, many of which were made by local actors caught up in two quagmires that Said spent a lifetime trying to expose: the asymmetrical web of U.S. power and the despicable ignorance and indifference of Washington's approach to the Middle East.

Articulated in a relentless stream of articles, interviews, and public addresses published in the United States, Europe, and the Middle East throughout the 1990s and the early years of the twenty-first century, Said's critique of two seminal and related aspects of the Oslo process stands out as particularly memorable and valid. One is the relationship instigated by the process between Arafat's political elite and Israel. The other is the morally, politically, and materially corrupt Palestinian protostate that ensued.

Said was quick to recognize that the regime of Israeli-Palestinian relations created by the Oslo accord turned the newly formed Palestinian Authority (PA) into a subcontractor for Israeli security. He also realized that this put the PA on a clear collision course with the interests and instincts of the nation-building and state-building efforts of the Palestinian national movement. One has only to read the statements regularly issued nowadays by Hamas and similar dissenting Arab and Islamist voices in Iraq, Saudi Arabia, Afghanistan, and around Osama bin Laden against Arab regimes and agents accused of subordinating national interests to the demands of foreign occupying powers to realize the penetrating quality of Said's early assessment of the impasse the PA created for itself within the Oslo framework.

Said's consistent opposition to the Oslo agreement was as politically courageous as it was intellectually incisive. It combined his strengths in analyzing political and cultural elites, demonstrated so astutely in his academic preoccupations even before *Orientalism,* with insights into Arafat's immediate environment and style of governance that Said had gained a decade earlier. These strengths were augmented by the fiercely independent position Said maintained throughout his universe: in academia, in public intellectual arenas, in the United States, in Europe, and in the Arab world. In all of these contexts, his willingness to speak truth in the face of power produced a clear and deeply trusted voice of a kind one rarely finds in protracted conflictual situations and of a quality that is decidedly unique in the context of the Middle East conflict.

DAN RABINOWITZ is senior lecturer in the departments of sociology and anthropology at Tel Aviv University. He is the author of *Overlooking Nazareth: The Ethnography of Exclusion in a Mixed Town in Galilee* (1997).

This combination also positioned Said at the perfect vantage point and commentary position vis-à-vis the inner workings of Arafat's protostate in Palestine. Not surprisingly, Edward was among the first to realize and to expose the unacceptable norms that shaped the new regime and, through it, the reality of everyday life for so many Palestinians: the abuse of power, the convoluted structure and manipulative nature of the bureaucracy, the opaque and undemocratic political processes, the latifunds established by security chiefs and political apparatchiks in their attempts to milk the vast resources made available to the Palestinian people through the People-to-People initiatives funded by the European Union—all taking place simultaneously under the watchful but complacent eye of Israel.

Said's critique of the PA may have been fueled in part by his growing personal mistrust of Arafat, acquired at the period following the PNC resolution of 1988. It was at that crucial time, when the resolve of the Palestine Liberation Organization (PLO) to find a territorial compromise with Israel was being played out for the first time in real negotiations with the United States, that Said became aware of Arafat's unwillingness and incapacity to run a critically important political process in a coherent and effective manner. The worst part, Said once intimated, was the lack of personal integrity and the devious manner in which Arafat maneuvered PLO officials he himself deployed, thus defeating the very purpose they were collectively trying to achieve.

The sobering lucidity with which Said deflated the euphoria following Oslo created a credible and timely alternative. Its persuasiveness stemmed from its inherent logic but also from the easily recognizable fact that Said had no hidden agenda. He was a public intellectual seeking a better and more just future for his people.

This recap of Said's early critique of Oslo sets the stage for an analysis of two additional aspects of the process that have largely escaped many of those observing Israel/Palestine from the West. The first is the notion that the Oslo process signaled the beginning—not the end—of Israeli military occupation of the West Bank and Gaza. The second is the contribution of the 1990s and of the Oslo process to the militarization of Israeli politics and society.

Oslo and the Belated Military Occupation

Soon after taking power in 1992, Yitzhak Rabin and Shimon Peres began responding to the first Palestinian intifada, the 1988 resolution of the PNC, and the Madrid conference of 1991—and to the de facto recognition of Israel that the latter two entailed. Rabin and Peres led Israel and Israelis to a historic acceptance of the PLO as a legitimate manifestation of the Palestinian national movement. This necessary step toward genuine reconciliation assumed practical form in the series of handovers of territory from Israeli control to Palestinian rule that took place on the ground between 1994 and 1996.

The Palestinians, while not unanimous, were clear about their vision of the goal for the process: a viable independent state in the territories occupied by Israel since 1967, with East Jerusalem as its capital. Rabin, on the other hand, consistently refused to commit to any long-term view of where the Oslo process was likely to lead. For example, unlike some of his cabinet ministers, for example, he never uttered the expression "a Palestinian state." The Israeli public as well as those around him were kept guessing. Peres, while more outspoken, did not provide a clearer formula either as Rabin's foreign minister or as his immediate stand-in after the assassination.

In this absence of a political vision, the Israeli military was left to its own devices to shape its immediate and future moves every time a tract was handed over to the Palestinians. The generals, headed by Ehud Barak as chief of staff, filled this conceptual vacuum in a manner one might expect from military strategists. Using a worse-case scenario as their baseline, they treated every inch of territory handed over to the Palestinians as a potential springboard for future attacks on Israel. Barak, who was then and is now explicitly suspicious of the Palestinians generally and the Oslo process particularly, made the Israeli Defense Forces (IDF) back up each pullout with meticulous planning and elaborate construction; the tracts handed over were surrounded by new bypass roads and roadblocks, new military camps and observation points. The perimeters of Israeli settlements were expanded, and tighter control of the neighboring civilian Palestinian communities became the order of the day.

The result was a tragic paradox, which most Palestinians are all too conscious of but which many in the West utterly fail to recognize. Instead of ending the military occupation of the territories, as the Palestinians first expected, the Oslo process soon became an instrument for enhancing it.

Between 1967 and 2000, Israel's military control of the West Bank and Gaza was rather loose. The IDF was deployed primarily on the outer perimeter of the territories, mainly facing outward to Jordan and to Egypt. The underlying principle was to disengage from the civilian population as much as possible; Israel employed a largely civilian administration to perform governmental tasks and duties. Direct military presence was, to use Frantz Fanon's suggestive conceptualization, assumed rather than experienced, a cardboard facade representing a readily available but otherwise invisible and distant force.

This was reflected, incidentally, in the dubious status the Occupied Territories were accorded within the ranks of the IDF before 2000. Deployment in the Occupied Territories was treated as nonoperational duty, often signaling the beginning of the end of a professional officer's career.

The Oslo process turned all this on its head. The handover of major towns in the West Bank and Gaza to Palestinian control was supposed to be accompanied by the transfer of administrative responsibility to Palestinian institutions. Instead, the IDF now defined its duties anew to fit its own precautionary attitude to territorial handover. The old mission statement formulated for it in 1968 by Moshe Dayan—namely, to keep out of Palestinian towns and let the Palestinians live their lives as normally as possible—was out, and the IDF began to operationalize its treatment of Palestinian civilians in terms of preemptive and retaliatory responses to a perceived potential military threat. The redeployment was repeatedly accompanied by the encircling of Palestinian towns with installations, as I have described above, but also by the drafting of detailed contingency plans for rapid intervention, involving heavy machinery, should Palestinian hostility indeed erupt. A powerful cycle of self-fulfilling prophecies was put in motion, which came to full fruition in late 2000. The military occupation of Palestinian life in the West Bank and Gaza was on. Three of its elements have since had exposure on the internet and, to a lesser extent, in printed and electronic media in the West: the apartheid road system; the new Israeli roadblocks, designed to limit Palestinians' everyday movement to a sluggish minimum; and the regime of travel permits that, even when issued by the PA, are closely monitored by Israel.

The belated military occupation of the West Bank and Gaza accounts for the dramatic difference between the first intifada and the current one. In the first one, friction with the IDF was limited, as the army was distant from the urban scenery. In the second intifada, fortified IDF posts right outside most Palestinian towns have become foci of attacks by outraged youngsters that quickly deteriorate to exchanges of gunfire. With the Israeli army so well prepared in terms of fortification, equipment, strategy, and tactics, no wonder it has sustained so few casualties from direct Palestinian attacks. Consequently, many Palestinians feel that the Camp David summit in July 2000 was an Israeli ploy to present the Palestinians with an unacceptable formula, provoke them to a militant response, and unleash the IDF to clamp down on them with force. Whether or not such deviousness on the part of the Israeli government was indeed the case, the discrepancy between the high hopes of freedom and independence Palestinians developed in early 1994 as Arafat returned from exile to head the newly established PA and the realities of the unprecedented military occupation that ensued was nothing short of debilitating.

Oslo and the Advanced Militarization of Israel

But Oslo and its inevitable collapse since 2000 facilitated another disconcerting process: the creeping militarization of Israel. For that, we need to go back a century. The first decade of the twentieth century saw territorial Zionism crystallizing as a practical ethnoterritorial political project focused on the colonization of Palestine. Mainstream Zionism has since systematically and successfully dismissed all voices, Jewish and non-Jewish, that advocate alternative trajectories. One of the elements in this Zionist trajectory has been the development and valorization by mainstream Zionism of a military prowess ostensibly designed to shield a national project that enjoys moral legitimacy and international support. As the twentieth century progressed, however, this element of Zionism ran out of control. Now, in the early years of the twenty-first century, the military force of Israel is no longer an instrument; it has grown to be a goal unto itself, a universe that follows its own logic. It now in many ways defines the state, shapes most of its policies, and colors the worldview of many of its citizens. For example, it is famously manifest in the way mainstream political parties in Israel prefer that their leadership positions be held by retired generals. Voters follow suit obediently, most recently with the election of Ehud Barak as leader of the Labor party and prime minister in 1999 and in the overwhelming popular support for Ariel Sharon in the elections in 2001 and 2003.

The 1990s were fateful in this respect. While the IDF had been careful not to become embroiled in party politics or in direct power brokerage, it nevertheless became involved in geopolitics through its interpretation of the Oslo process in ways hitherto unknown. This was complicated further by the Israeli withdrawal from Lebanon in July 2000. Many on the political right and in the top brass of the IDF became convinced that the Arabs, having seen the IDF pushed out of Lebanon by a handful of Hezbollah zealots, now saw the IDF as vulnerable. They sought an opportunity to reassert authority and poise, and they got it in the only active military frontier still available for them—the Occupied Territories.

These trajectories were personified in Barak, the IDF chief of staff during the Oslo process, who in 1999 became prime minister and chief negotiator with the Palestinians. The dynamics of belated occupation and advanced militarization all came to their somber conclusion at Camp David and Taba in 2000 and early 2001.

At Camp David and Taba, Barak spun into existence a process he presented to the Israeli public and the world as "a moment of truth," one that was to "unveil the Palestinians" and "finally expose" their "real intentions." Claiming his proposition of a Palestinian state was unprecedented and unlikely ever to be repeated, he attributed the failure of the negotiations to the

Palestinians and accused them of having entered the Oslo process, almost a decade earlier, on false pretenses. If it is war they want, Barak proclaimed during the negotiations, we need to know it. Only then can we look the parents of our soldiers in the eye and tell them we did everything in our power to search for peace before we sent their children to battle. The Palestinians were once again ejected from legitimate politics and reinserted into the realm of terror.

This simplistic view is based on the dangerous notion, so ripe today in the mainstreams in Israel, the United States, and beyond, that liberal modernizing projects, often dubbed harbingers of "freedom," are a threat to others, particularly Muslims, to the extent of pushing them to take up terror. If this is so, this logic goes, the West's response can be either to get tough or to lose everything. This, of course, underwrites a virtually unlimited license to use military power in the name of "security" in the defense of "freedom."

My critique, which has its roots in Edward Said's ideas on Israel/Palestine as formulated during the Oslo process, diverges from the view most people have of why the Oslo process collapsed in flames in the fall of 2000. Rather than identifying Oslo as the voice of reason that unfortunately got derailed by irresponsible and irrational leaderships, it sees Oslo as inherently flawed. In the final analysis, the Oslo process could have emerged as it did only against the backdrop of the vast misapprehensions and indifference that characterize most Western readings of the Palestinians and the Middle East—the very misapprehensions Edward Said was so brilliantly outspoken about throughout his life.

The Question of Zionism: Continuing the Dialogue

Jacqueline Rose

'Why should the Palestinians make the effort to understand Zionism?' The question came from a young woman in the audience at one of the many memorials held for you, this one in London last November under the auspices of the *London Review of Books*. It was not your priority, responded Ilan Pappé. And Sara Roy simply and powerfully told the anecdote of how she had witnessed Palestinians flooding with joy onto the curfewed streets of the West Bank where she was living when the possibility of a Palestinian state was first acknowledged by Israel, while the soldiers stood by in silence and just watched. There will be understanding enough, I heard her saying, when there is justice.

They were of course both right; your preoccupation was with justice. In one of your most irate pieces about the occupation—'Sober Truths about Israel and Zionism', written for *Al-Ahram* and *Al-Hayat* in 1995, when the bitter reality of post-Oslo was becoming clearer by the day—you mince no words about the cruel asymmetry of the conflict and the peculiar injustice of the settlements: what they tell us about Israel as a nation, about Zionism as its founding idea. Once a piece of land is confiscated, 'it belongs to "the land of Israel"' and is 'officially restricted for the exclusive use of Jews'. Many nations including the United States, you allow, were founded on the confiscation of land, but no other country then designates this land for the sole use of one portion of its citizens. You are citing Israel Shahak, Holocaust survivor, founder of the Israeli League of Human Rights, 'one of the small handful of Israeli Jews who tells the truth *as it is*'.[1]

1. Edward W. Said, 'Sober Truths about Israel and Zionism' (1995), *Peace and Its Discontents: Essays on Palestine in the Middle East Peace Process* (New York, 1995), p. 129; hereafter abbreviated 'ST'.

Earlier in the essay, you tell the anecdote of a Palestinian student at Birzeit University who, at the end of a lecture in which you were advocating a more 'scientific and precise' approach on the part of the Arab world to understanding the United States, raised his hand to say 'that it was a more disturbing fact that no such programs existed in Palestine for the study of Israel' (anticipating in reverse the young woman in London) ('ST', p. 128). Shahak is your answer. Understanding Israel means understanding the discriminatory foundations of the nation-state:

> Unless we recognise the real issue—which is the racist character of the Zionist Movement and the State of Israel and the roots of that racism in the Jewish religious law [Halacha]—we will not be able to understand our realities. And unless we can understand them, we will not be able to change them. [Quoted in 'ST', p. 130]

If that was all you had to say, if you had had just that much to say, you would have already been saying, and so fully in character, so much. This is speaking truth to power—'*as it is*'—a truth rarely acknowledged in Israel's self-representation, still less to the outside world. My only question would be to that last line of Shahak's: does speaking this particular truth, which is indeed heard today both inside and outside the country, make it more easy to change, or is it driving Israel, yet again on the defensive, ever more fiercely to entrench itself?

And, yet, to stop there is not, I believe—and I believe you believed—to go far enough. Your view was more complex. In fact you decried the UN resolution equating Zionism with racism as politically counterproductive: 'I was never happy with the resolution'.[2] Significantly, given your call for scientific precision in understanding, it was not *precise* enough: '*Racism* is too vague a term: Zionism is Zionism'.[3] 'The question of Zionism', you said in conversation with Salman Rushdie in 1986, 'is the touchstone of contemporary political judgment.'[4] What did you mean?

2. Said, 'What People in the U.S. Know about Islam Is a Stupid Cliché' (1992), interview with Hasan M. Jafri, *Power, Politics, and Culture: Interviews with Edward W. Said*, ed. Gauri Viswanathan (London, 2004), p. 378.

3. Said, *The Question of Palestine* (1979; New York, 1992), p. 112; hereafter abbreviated *QP*.

4. Said, 'On Palestinian Identity: A Conversation with Salman Rushdie' (1986), *The Politics of Dispossession: The Struggle for Palestinian Self-Determination, 1969–1994* (London, 1994), p. 121.

JACQUELINE ROSE is professor of English at Queen Mary University of London. Her books include *The Haunting of Sylvia Plath, States of Fantasy, On Not Being Able to Sleep: Psychoanalysis and the Modern World,* and her novel, *Albertine*. She was the writer and presenter of the Channel 4 TV documentary 'A Dangerous Liaison—Israel and America'. *The Question of Zion,* first delivered as the Christian Gauss seminars at Princeton University in 2003, will be published in spring 2005.

Speaking at the memorial in November, I had cited what remains for me one of your most poignant pleas: 'We cannot coexist as two communities of detached and uncommunicatingly separate suffering'—the 'we' performing the link for which it appeals.[5] I cannot remember whether it was this quotation or my later attempt in the discussion to talk about Zionism that provoked the question of the young woman from the floor. But for me it is the peculiar quality and gift of your thought that you could make your denunciation of the injustice of Israel towards the Palestinians, while also speaking—without ever softening the force of that critique—if not quite *for*, nonetheless *of* the reality of the other side: what drove Israel, how it had come to be, what makes it what it is now.

Perhaps your best known discussion of Zionism is the chapter in *The Question of Palestine* (1979), which was your first extended analysis of this history, famously entitled 'Zionism from the Standpoint of Its Victims'; the title unambiguously announces that your priority is to raise the plight of the Palestinians, at the time more or less passed over in silence, both in the world and for themselves. Yet that objective, on which you never wavered, is already here accompanied by interconnections and diffusions of another kind. You were, after all, both a political thinker and a literary critic (the two roles passionately, intimately joined). 'The task of criticism, or, to put it another way, the role of the critical consciousness in such cases', you write in the course of the chapter, 'is to be able to make distinctions, to produce differences where at present there are none' (*QP*, p. 59). To critique Zionism is not, you insisted then, anti-Semitic (an assertion that critics of Israel, especially post 9/11, are forced to make even more loudly today). It is, in one of your favourite formulae of Gramsci's, to make an inventory of the historical forces that have made anyone—a people—who they are. Zionism needs to be read. What is required is a critical consciousness that dissects the obdurate language of the present by delving into the buried fragments of the past, to produce differences 'where at present there are none'. It is not therefore a simple political identity that you are offering the Palestinians on whose behalf you speak nor a simple version of the seemingly intractable reality to which they find themselves opposed. It is rather something more disorienting that confers and troubles identity at one and the same time (if the past is never a given nor, once uncovered, is it ever merely a gift).

For me, Gramsci's injunction always contained a psychoanalytic demand: '"the consciousness of what one really is . . . is 'knowing thyself'"', although such knowledge is hardly easy, as every psychoanalyst will attest (*QP*, p. 73). I see this as your injunction to Zionism and Palestinian na-

---

5. Said, 'Bases for Coexistence' (1997), *The End of the Peace Process–Oslo and After* (London, 2000), p. 208.

tionalism alike. By the time we get to 'Bases for Coexistence' in 1997, to this classic Freudian dictum, you have added another no less painful and difficult dimension: 'We cannot coexist as two communities of detached and uncommunicatingly separate suffering'. And then, against the grain of your own and your people's sympathies, 'There is suffering and injustice enough for everyone'.[6] (After this piece was published in *Al-Hayat* and *Al-Ahram*, you received your first hate mail in the Arab press.) Not just self-reflective, nor just internally unsettling, but perhaps precisely because it is both of these, such knowledge has the power to shift the boundaries between peoples. There can be no progress in the Middle East, I hear you saying, without a shared recognition of pain.

As I reread you today on Zionism, this strained, complicated demand seems in fact a type of constant. This may be of course because I personally so want and need it to be (as Brecht notoriously acknowledged when asked whether his interpretation of *Coriolanus* was true to Shakespeare's meaning; he was both 'reading *in* and reading *into*' the play). But it seems to me that—contrary to your detractors—you were always trying to do two things at once that you knew to be well-nigh impossible. It was as if you were requiring all critics of Israel—whether Arab and Jewish and without dissolving the real historical and political differences between the two peoples—to hold together in our hearts and minds the polar opposite emotions of empathy and rage (however reluctant the first, however legitimate the second for your people might be). Today the understanding of Zionism seems an even more crucial task than when you made the question the touchstone of political judgement nearly twenty years ago. I want to place the role of the critic as you defined it in 1979 together with the plea for a shared recognition of suffering of 1997 on either side of your answer to the Palestinian student at Birzeit. What then do we see?

Zionism has been a success. You said this many times. Shocking, given the catastrophe for the Palestinians, but true—even for those, such as David Grossman and Yaakov Perry, former head of Shin Bet (to mention just two), who see Israel today as in a perhaps irreversible decline, in thrall to a militarism destructive of the Palestinians and of itself. Historically Israel has fulfilled its aims. You repeat the point in an interview with Hasan M. Jafri for the *Karachi Herald* as late as 1992: 'Zionism for the Jew was a wonderful thing. They say it was their liberation movement. They say it was that which gave them sovereignty. They finally had a homeland'.[7] But, as you laid it out so clearly in 'Zionism from the Standpoint of Its Victims', Zionism suffers

6. Ibid., p. 207.
7. Said, 'What People in the U.S. Know about Islam Is a Stupid Cliché', p. 378.

from an internal 'bifurcation' (*QP*, p. 87) or even, to push the psychoanalytic vocabulary one stage further, splitting: 'between care for the Jews and an almost total disregard for the non-Jews or native Arab population' (*QP*, p. 83). Not only unjust, this splitting is self-defeating for the Israeli nation. In the eyes of the Arabs, Zionism becomes nothing other than an unfolding design 'whose deeper roots in Jewish history and the terrible Jewish experience was necessarily obscured by what was taking place before their eyes' (*QP*, p. 83). Freud of course spoke of the 'blindness of the seeing eye' (or in the words of Jean-Luc Godard, 'shut your eyes, and *see*'). Zionism, we could say, has done itself a major disservice. So fervently has it nourished the discrimination between Jew and non-Jew, the rationale of its dispossession of the Palestinians, that, while it may have seized the earth, it has also snatched the grounds for understanding from beneath its own feet.

This is not, of course, an apology for Israel; that much must be clear. It is more that the Palestinian cause has been weakened by its failure to understand the *inner* force of what it is up against (as Lenin once famously remarked, you should always construct your enemy at their strongest point). The 'internal cohesion and solidity' of Zionism has completely 'eluded the understanding of Arabs' (*QP*, p. 88), as has the 'intertwined terror and the exultation' out of which it was born—or in other words 'what Zionism meant for Jews' (*QP*, p. 66). It is the affective dimension, as it exerts its pressure historically, that has been blocked from view. You are analysing a trauma—'an immensely traumatic Zionist effectiveness' (*QP*, p. 83). Terror, exultation, trauma—Zionism has the ruthlessness of the symptom (it is the symptom of its own success). Given this emphasis, your unexpected and rarely commented remarks on the 'benevolent', 'humanistic' impulse of Zionism towards its own people are even more striking (there is no one- or even two-dimensionality here). You never ceased to insist on the colonial nature of the venture, and the cruel Orientalism of how the Arab people were treated and portrayed. But what if the key to understanding the catastrophe for the Palestinians, of 1948 and after, were to be found in the love that the Jewish people—for historically explicable reasons—lavish on themselves?

We have entered the most stubborn and self-defeating psychic terrain, where a people can be loving and lethal, and their most exultant acts towards—and triumph over—an indigenous people expose them to the dangers they most fear. For it is not just of course that Israel's conduct has made it impossible for the Arabs to understand her nor that Israel has been blind towards the Arabs (in fact never true), but that she sees things in the wrong place: 'Everything that did stay to challenge Israel was viewed not as something *there*, but as a sign of something *outside* Israel and Zionism bent on its destruction—from the outside' (*QP*, p. 89). Israel is vulnerable because it cannot see the people who—whether in refugee camps on the borders (the putative Palestinian state), or inside the country (the Israeli-Arabs), or scattered all over the world (the Palestinian diaspora)—are in fact, psychically as well as politically, *in its midst*.

Contrast this again, as you do repeatedly, with Israel as a nation for *all* Jewish people—this passionately inclusive, and violently excluding, embrace. Here time and place are infinite:

> If every Jew in Israel represents "the whole Jewish people"—which is a population made up not only of the Jews in Israel, but also of generations of Jews who existed in the past (of whom the present Israelis are the remnant) and those who exist in the future, as well as those who live elsewhere.
>
> Israel would not be simply the state of its citizens (which included Arabs, of course) but the state of "the whole Jewish people," having a kind of sovereignty over land and peoples that no other state possessed or possesses. [*QP*, pp. 104, 84]

This is in fact far worse than merely 'two communities . . . of uncommunicatingly separate suffering' which might suggest indifference or ignorance of a more straightforward kind. This is a historically embedded failure of vision—multiply determined and with multiple, self-perpetuating effects. In these early readings, you delve into the past, telling all the parties that the main critical and political task is to understand how and why.

I realise now that my writing on Zionism is an extended footnote to your questions, an attempt to enter into the 'terror and the exultation' out of which Zionism was born, to grasp what you so aptly term the 'immensely traumatic Zionist effectiveness' of the Israeli nation-state. You mean of course traumatic for the Palestinians. I would add also for the Jews (exultation does not dispel fear). But I have also wanted to revive the early Jewish voices—Martin Buber, Hans Kohn, Hannah Arendt, and Ahad Haam, some of whom called themselves Zionists—who sounded the critique, uttered the warnings that have become all the more prescient today. Somewhere, I believe, Zionism had the self-knowledge for which Gramsci and, through him, you make your plea, although I know in the case of Buber and Arendt you feel they were not finally equal to their critique. Calling up these voices, torn from the pages of a mostly forgotten past, I like to think that—as well as rebuilding the legacy of my own Jewish history—I am also doing what you would have wanted, fulfilling a very personal demand from you to me.

We did not of course always agree. I am sure that in the last analysis you

believed that entering the Zionist imagination might be risking one identification too far (are you writing an apology? you once asked). I was pre-
paring the Christian Gauss seminars to be delivered September 2003 under
the title 'The Question of Zion', a deliberate echo of, and my tribute to, *The
Question of Palestine*. When I was writing them that summer, you wanted
to read them, but I needed to finish them first. 'I might be able to help you',
you said. It was July, and we were sitting in your favourite London hotel
with your son, Wadie, and his wife, Jennifer, arguing about Zionism while
violins played their accompaniment to afternoon tea.

You were planning to attend the second lecture, but knowing by the time
of my visit that you might not be well enough, I hurriedly emailed them to
my neighbour here before I left so they could be sent to your personal as-
sistant, Sandra Fahy, who was always so helpful, just in case. Then, as happens, something was wrong with the attachments, so they could not be sent
when you asked for them. I arrived at your apartment clutching a rapidly
photocopied version when I visited you on the Sunday four days before you
died. Amongst many other things, we talked about the dreadful, deterio-
rating situation in Israel/Palestine—a decline that had so cruelly tracked
your illness over the past decade. 'I will read them this afternoon', you said
at the end. You were admitted to the hospital the next day. It was of course
the conversation I most wanted to have. I had held back in the blithe belief
that our dialogue would be endless, that having defeated your illness so
many many times before you would go on doing so forever. I will not have
the gift of your response to the lectures. Which is doubtless why I have used
this occasion to lift out of your work the inspiration and form of their imagining.

Thinking about Edward Said: Pages from a Memoir

Gayatri Spivak

When I had contracted with the University of Massachusetts Press—in 1967 or 1968—to translate *De la grammatologie,* my editor sent me a copy of Edward Said's "*Abecedarium culturae:* Structuralism, Absence, Writing" that had just appeared in *TriQuarterly* and was later included as a chapter in *Beginnings.* It must have been 1971. Later that year I found out that my contract was with Hopkins and that J. Hillis Miller, who was then at Yale, and had already started organizing Derrida's U.S. career, had something to do with it. I never solved that puzzle. The editor at Massachusetts had stuck a note on the article, something like, What on earth is going on here? Perhaps he was beginning to realize, in giving me a contract for translating and introducing Jacques Derrida, that the press had bitten off more than it could chew.

Well, I read the piece. I had ordered Derrida off a catalogue, on impulse, not knowing his name, or anything about the French scene. It was a sort of self-help project, to which I still subscribe, shamefacedly. I have no general education, whereas Edward's piece seemed to be incredibly knowledgeable in just that way. I read the piece carefully, made notes in the margin, and filed it.

Those years were full of turmoil in my personal life, but I kept translating Derrida and kept teaching the "poststructuralists," who were all still writing. (I think I invented that ugly and imprecise word, a few years later, in my introduction to the *Grammatology.*) I sometimes think I developed a sort of comradeship with them precisely because I was so untutored, plugging away in remote Iowa City. "French" feminism, contained in the red covers of Elaine Marks and Isabelle de Courtivron's book, appearing in 1980, was a different matter entirely. The opening pages of this memoir, trying to touch my foremothers, will give a sense of the distance between that feminism and whatever I might call mine.

1971. I was to meet Derrida for the first time later that year. I am looking at my notes on Edward's article. Remember, I didn't know him or know of him either. I was not under his spell, as I later would be, like anyone who met him. I was only a dogged translator learning on the job, a patient and transfixed reader. I noticed this American's (nothing in the piece gave any other clue) impatient mistranslations. (It was much later that I would come to realize that this charming impatience was part of his signature.)

"Nothingness" for *anéantissement,* for example. That way, the ontology of annihilation could be rewritten as the "ontology of nothingness." Foucault's bold reversal of the process character of ontology—the philosophy that studies (coming into) being—could thus be controlled by way of a neat Sartrian displacement, moving the cursor to the second noun on Jean-Paul's title: *Being and Nothingness.* "Paralyze" for *trahir*—"betray"—so that a way of being meaning-ful without controlling meaning—carrying meaning, betraying it for others to read—could be presented as a general incapacity. "Significant" for *signifiant*—"signifier," of course; "non-conscious" for *inconscient*—"unconscious," of course; "the conditions and the forms of its contents" for *les conditions de ses formes et de ses contenus,* a real philosophical gaffe; and many more. "This smart man wants these people to mean something and he won't let them mean what they say—he is too impatient, he won't give them a chance," I wrote in the margin where Edward had written "structuralism is good public relations these days." It now seems inconceivable that he followed Steven Marcus in thinking that Foucault believed in dissociation of sensibility!

Translation is the most intimate act of reading. By then I was tight with grammatology. Looking at the notes now, it amuses me to see how much Edward was turned off by Derrida; Derrida's was exactly not his kind of charisma.

My supervisor at Cornell had been Paul de Man. From Cornell, he had moved to Johns Hopkins. In the early seventies, he and Hillis Miller moved to Yale and "the Yale school" got its start. Derrida got a visiting professorship contract there, and I went to Yale for as many of his lectures as I could.

1974 was a memorable year. At Yale I met both Edward Said and Jacques Lacan. I had not retained the name of the man who wrote "*Abecedarum*

GAYATRI SPIVAK, Avalon Foundation Professor in the Humanities and director of the Center for Comparative Literature and Society at Columbia University, teaches English and the politics of culture. Her most recent book is *Chotli Munda and His Asnow* (2002).

culturae." I did not connect it to the Byronic figure sitting alone all the way down on a narrow bit of vista that the old Naples Pizza in New Haven allowed. "Do you know him?" de Man asked and, when I said no, he said, "You should. He works on Foucault." De Man introduced us, then and there.

Our friendship prospered, mostly on the phone. I didn't read anything else by him for a long time. It was Palestine that we talked about and I was, of course, convinced. Some years ago, I had thrown myself heart and soul into the Bangladesh conflict. Strangely enough, I was even then unmoved by Indian nationalism. It seemed too grandiose, too much identified with great men and women in my immediate past. And, as a citizen, I was more critical of India's policy than otherwise, especially because, a year into my friendship with Edward, Indira Gandhi declared martial law and the young people joining the Naxalbari movement—a movement where peasants and intellectuals made common cause against rural and urban corruption and exploitation—were often tortured and murdered. I couldn't interest Edward in Indian politics. To the end this remained my regret. He was of course interested in India's struggle for independence and figures such as Gandhi and Nehru. He was immediately forthcoming when I asked him to write an introduction for *Selected Subaltern Studies* in 1987. He got on well with Ranajit Guha, founding editor of the collective. He was certainly friendly with the South Asians and South Asianists in and around Columbia. He regularly cotaught with Akeel Bilgrami.

Towards the end of his life, he and Mariam went to India, where Edward received two doctorates. His account of the trip to me did not seem to come from the friend who knew my deep and little-advertised concern for social justice in India. Early on in our friendship, looking back upon himself critically, he had described himself as a "playboy" before he woke up to the question of Palestine. (Who knows where one's stereotypes for oneself are hatched?) That word came to mind as I heard him speak about India. At any rate, our friendship (by then carried on as if Columbia University did not exist) received a dent from this. I was uneasy. In a while I sent word to him through our common friend Jacqueline Rose during what turned out to be the last days. He sent this back: "Ask Gayatri to make a gesture." There wasn't time.

But I am getting ahead of myself. During those early days, it was all about Palestine. I made speeches when asked and met interesting people, of whom I remember now Ibrahim Abu-Lughod, Nubar Hovsepian, and, of course, Eqbal Ahmed. In fact, the South Asia thing had an innocent repercussion there. Edward was political about Pakistan, as the eastern edge of West Asia (read, Middle East). He wrote not only for *Al-Ahram* (Cairo) and *Al-Hayat* (Arab journal out of London) but also for *Dawn*, the English-language Pakistani journal. But in that group of West Asians, Eqbal's Arabic was joshed a bit, in an altogether good-humored way, for its South Asian accent. He would turn to me and speak in Bengali, my mother tongue. For we were both born before the subcontinent was divided, and he was born in Purnia, in the neighboring state of Bihar, not very far from my hometown.

In those days I met Edward mostly at conferences. I remember "Politics of Interpretation" at the University of Chicago in 1981, where he made the important statement, in response to a particularly inept question, that he would be the first critic of the Palestinian state once it was established. (Later, I admired his principled stand against the beleaguered Arafat. Yet, with infinite political tact, he wrote little against the chairman except in the pages of *Al-Ahram,* whereas the so-called Oslo peace accords encountered his well-reasoned anger. Joseph Massad tells me that it was after Oslo that Edward got radicalized. That may well be. Even I understood that the false promise of Oslo started from a recoding of the situation of Israel—from a racist state to the only democracy in the Middle East.) Just recently, John Carlos Rowe has reminded us in the pages of the *American Quarterly* that I had taken Edward to task for not having sufficient sympathy for feminism, but I don't remember that. I did always remind him of feminism, remind him not to "take care of it" by making it one item on a list of worthy causes, or being nice to women, but that was between him and me. Am I right in thinking that he acknowledged at least my tenaciousness by telling the *New York Times* that I was the best postcolonial feminist?

Another big conference was the one at Essex, not "Europe and Its Others," but another one. I remember nothing of it but Edward and me walking across a sunlit grassy slope, a step ahead of Talal Asad, whom I had just met. Edward ruffled my hair and said, "We are on show here." At a conference in Marquette, he "played for me" on a hopelessly out-of-tune piano in the corner of the hall. I will never forget those sweet moments. I think it was a way of presenting alliance in those days when it did not exist in the United States academy between people from different parts of Asia. Also, it was just a way of enjoying those gigs. We were not jaded yet. He would give me advice on clothes, as I'm sure he gave many of his friends. He told me to stop wearing saris, and he was right, I think. It turns people off. But I was scared of reformatting my body for Western clothes alone, and things remained the same.

Our friendship prospered on the conference circuit. Not too many people thought the way we were thinking then. The postcolonial faction was not yet clearly distinguished from the theory crowd. I used to say that I was the chick vocalist on the theory-performing band: Stanley Fish, Fred Jameson, Edward Said, Hayden White, give or take a few; but I was always there.

It was at the School of Criticism at Northwestern in 1982 that our friendship thickened. It seems portentous now. Something began and something ended. That was the last time I saw de Man. He came to my apartment, helped me pack—he was an immensely generous and nonhierarchical gossipy man (I was gobsmacked by the wartime letters when they were shown to me in an attic in Belgium five years later)—and walked me—somewhere, I forget, bus station? It is the leave-taking in the middle of the street that I remember, and remember thinking, the whites of his eyes are yellow! I took off for Britain and came back a few days later. He had collapsed and been flown back to New Haven, soon to be diagnosed with liver cancer.

That was the time of the Israeli massacre of the Palestinian refugees in Sabra and Shatila. Edward felt alone, surrounded by colleagues whose minds were occupied with the here and now of the school, with the politics of the academy. We were an island of two. He talked, I listened.

And so it went. We did public appearances together, for Palestine. In 1983, at the "Marxist Interpretation of Culture" conference in Champaign-Urbana, he could not himself attend, but suggested that we invite a man who had formerly worked for the Bertrand Russell Foundation to speak on behalf of Palestine. I came to New York often, saw him, had long conversations. I remember them all, but two or three occasions stand out. Once he was enraged. A colleague had accused him of anti-Semitism because he had called Farrakhan "a Black Begin." Mariam came in in the middle of this conversation, and Edward pointed an agitated finger at me—"Ask her, ask her!" I remember Mariam completely deflecting the conversation and calming him down by taking it away from the entire dispute, saying, "She has a name!" Another time, in December of 1985, it was his fiftieth birthday. Mariam was cooking a meat dish in the kitchen. I had come in from out of town hoping I could have lunch with Edward. "See if you can get him to go to lunch," said Mariam. "It is his fiftieth birthday. He is so angry at being fifty that he refuses to go to dinner with me." Of course we did not go to lunch. I exchanged a few pleasantries with a gloomy Edward and went off to eat alone.

When I think of that day now I also think of the way he acknowledged his last, long, drawn-out illness. I remember his son, Wadie, mentioning that when speech left him, he was still rolling his eyes humorously at the moaning and groaning of the patient in the next bed. This stark contrast of impatience with friends and family, combined with great courage, was a characteristic of Edward Said.

I recall two particular instances of his support. In 1982 I managed to get a job offer from a reputable university in the U.S. Southeast. An embittered applicant had said to him: "She got it because she is a Third World woman." And Edward: "Not on that level." In 1988, when a couple of younger colleagues trashed me as a racist because of a protocol mistake, Edward sent a message on his own, saying, "Gayatri works for the oppressed, stop this." I was immensely grateful that he had somehow drawn me into what was surely his life—working for the oppressed.

I came to Pittsburgh in 1986. "You're inching your way to the East Coast," he said. I took it with a laugh, as I had to take the dry, sly, acute humor he kept reserved for friends.

I think he often thought I was a fool, to be so persuaded by "theory." His stand, as president of the Modern Language Association, against pretentious and obscure language was against me as well. I think I tried his patience precisely because he cared. I sat next to him on the plane coming back from the Chicago MLA, where he had excoriated unnamed but easily recognizable persons who wrote fatuously obscure books. I asked him why he had so trashed me at the MLA; it was transparent. He said, altogether unconvincingly, and he knew it as he said it, that it wasn't about me—and he named an eminent "French feminist." And he was amused by my on-the-ground political commitments that had to be different from his, for they were "post"-colonial. "The first critic of the state of Palestine," I had heard him say in 1981. My idea of practical usefulness—I was no stateswoman—was to show the state the usefulness of a different kind of teacher training for the largest sector of the electorate. It seemed such a difficult project, so different from most literacy or science efforts, that I kept quiet about this for the first ten years or so and finally opened my mouth by a happenstance that I will describe in my memoirs. So, anyway, when Edward would ask, "Gayatri, what *do* you do when you go to those villages?" I would give the usual answer, "Hang out" (*Mitwegsein,* suspend previous training in order to train yourself, *you* know). The answer was not satisfactory.

These differences in intellectual style fostered our friendship. Until I came to Columbia, in 1991. We were not just ourselves any longer, but also connected to groups. And his connections had history. I was never the Saids' guest once I settled in New York. Yet something lingered, in private conversations, sometimes political, sometimes not. I have tried to give you a sense of whatever it was that moved us to con-verse, to turn together.

When I came to Columbia, I had already taught full-time for twenty-six years, moved up though the ranks, mostly at state universities, but for Emory (and I didn't like it there). I'd said to the Columbia student newspaper when I arrived that I had not taught at an elite school and did not know how I would fare. Edward thought that was disingenuous. Columbia was his element; he began and ended his forty-year teaching career here. I am still learning how to build at Columbia, inching toward effectiveness, I hope.

These pages are part of a memoir that, according to Tariq Ali at least, Edward said I should write. I have called the book, *If Only . . .* , translating a phrase from Assia Djebar's wonderful essay "Forbidden Gaze, Severed Sound." The title seems particularly apposite when I think of the walk I walked with Edward W. Said.

Now that he is dead, people about whom he was at best dubious, and mere sycophants, tell us about the political discussions he had with them. The celebrated dead belong to everyone. I have said only personal things. Intellectually, I wanted to fill out his view of the secular intellectual precisely from the from-above/from-below differences that I recounted a bit ago. That essay has found its place in the "secularism" issue of *Boundary 2,* edited by Edward's beloved student Aamir Mufti. And I will read the phrase "relative autonomy," with reference to art, that is in his posthumous book *Humanism and Democratic Criticism* when there is a moment between deadlines.

Otherwise I chant that wild hymn, from the time when Hinduism was nearly indistinguishable from animism: as the ripe fruit bursts its skin, so immortality bursts out of death. In the love of family and friends, the intellectual journey of students. But also, harshly, literally, pushing up the daisies. In the face of that harsh immortality, the heart must break.

Maestro

Daniel Barenboim

Translated by Kimberly Borchard

Edward Said was many things for many people, but in reality his was a musician's soul in the deepest sense of the word.

He wrote about important universal issues such as exile, politics, integration. However, the most surprising thing for me, as his friend and great admirer, was the realization that, on many occasions, he actually formulated ideas and reached conclusions through music; and, along the same lines, he saw music as a reflection of the ideas that he had regarding other issues.

This is one of the main reasons why I believe that Said was an extremely important figure. His journey through this world took place precisely at a time when the humanity of music, its human value, and the value of thought, the transcendence of the idea written in sounds, were and regrettably continue to be concepts in decline.

His fierce antispecialization led him to criticize very strongly, and in my opinion very fairly, the fact that musical education was becoming increasingly poor, not only in the United States—which, after all, had imported the music of old Europe—but also in the very countries that had produced music's greatest figures: for example, in Germany, which had produced Beethoven, Brahms, Wagner, Schumann, and many others, or in France, which had produced Debussy and Ravel. In all these countries, which had been the cradle of musical creation, musical education was in rapid decline. Furthermore, he perceived a sign that bothered him exceedingly, a perception that was to unite us very quickly: even when there was musical education it was carried out in a very specialized way. In the best of cases, young people were offered the opportunity to practice an instrument, to acquire inevitably necessary knowledge of theory, of musicology, and of everything that a musician needs professionally. But, at the same time, there existed a widespread and growing incomprehension of a simultaneously simple and complex problem, that is, the impossibility of articulating with words the content of a musical work. After all, if it were possible to express in words the content of one of Beethoven's symphonies, we would no longer have a need for that symphony. But the fact that it is impossible to express in words the music's content does not mean that there is no content. That is why I assert that the question is simultaneously simple and complex.

This is a tendency that leads to an impoverished and narrow specialization. In the case of outstanding talents, it results in mechanization of the instrument, and in the case of creation, it leads composers to an incapacity to express that very richness that the human being discovered the potential to express through sound.

The paradox consists in the fact that music is only sound, but sound, in itself, is not music. Therein lies Said's main idea as a musician who—on a biographical note—was also an excellent pianist. In recent years, due to his terrible illness, he was unable to maintain the level of physical energy necessary to play the piano. I remember many unforgettable times that we spent playing Schubert pieces for four hands. Two or three years ago, I had a concert at Carnegie Hall in New York, and he was going through a very difficult period of his illness. The concert was on a Sunday afternoon. Although he knew that I had arrived that very morning from Chicago, he showed up very early at rehearsal with a volume of Schubert's pieces for four hands. He told me: "Today I want us to play at least eight bars, not for the pleasure of playing, but because I need it to survive." As it is easy to imagine, at that moment, just in from the airport and with one hour of rehearsal before the afternoon's concert, what he was proposing to me was the last thing that could have interested me. But, as is always the case in life, when you teach, you learn, and when you give, you receive. And when you teach you learn

DANIEL BARENBOIM, currently the music director of the Chicago Symphony Orchestra, coauthored with Edward Said *Parallels and Paradoxes* (2002). In the same year they jointly received the Prince of Asturias Award for Concord in recognition of their endeavors towards peace. In 2004, Barenboim was awarded the Tolerance Prize by the Evangelische Akademie Tutzing, the Order of the Federal Republic of Germany by President Johannes Rau, the Buber-Rosenzweig Medal, the Wolf Prize for the Arts in the Knesset in Jerusalem, and the Haviva Reik Peace Award in Berlin. KIMBERLY BORCHARD currently teaches Spanish at the University of Chicago, where she is working towards her Ph.D. in Latin American colonial literature.

because the student asks questions that you no longer even ask yourself because they are part of the almost automatic thought process that each one of us develops. And, suddenly, the question addresses something that forces us to rethink it from its origin, from its very essence. That is why, in the same way, when you give you receive, because it is when you least expect it. To receive something, when one expects to receive it, is much less interesting. Why do I say this? Because I was there, and, really, the last thing I wanted to do was to play Schubert for four hands. Naturally, I did it, with the greatest pleasure, because my dear friend, whom I so admired and loved, asked me to do so. But when we played, with him, those few minutes of a Schubert rondo—an extremely beautiful piece, which was not, however, the deepest or most transcendent—I felt musically enriched in a completely unexpected way. That was Edward Said.

Said was interested in detail. Indeed, he understood perfectly that musical genius or musical talent requires tremendous attention to detail. The genius attends to detail as though it were the most important thing. And, in doing so, he does not lose sight of the big picture; rather, he manages to trace out that big picture. Because the big picture, in music as in thought, must be the result of the coordination of small details. For that reason, when he listened to or spoke of music, he focused his attention on the small details that many professionals have not even discovered.

He had a refined knowledge of the art of composition and orchestration. He knew that in the second act of *Tristan and Isolde* at a certain moment the horns withdraw behind the stage and, a couple bars later, the same musical note reemerges in the pit orchestra's clarinets. What a number of singers I have had the honor and pleasure of collaborating with on that piece who are unaware of that detail and look behind them to see where the sound is coming from! They don't know that the note is no longer coming from behind the stage, but rather from the pit. He took interest in these things and was concerned with the detail itself, the value of the whole notwithstanding, because he understood that this meticulous interest in detail conferred upon the whole a grandeur that it cannot acquire without this profound concern for detail.

He also knew how to distinguish clearly between power and force, which constituted one of the main ideas of his struggle. He knew quite well that, in music, force is not power, something that many of the world's political leaders do not perceive. The difference between power and force is equivalent to the difference between volume and intensity in music. When one speaks with a musician and says to him, "You are not playing intensely enough," his first reaction is to play louder. And it is exactly the opposite:

the lower the volume, the greater the need for intensity, and the greater the volume, the greater the need for a calm force in the sound.

These are some examples that illustrate my conviction that his concept of life and of the world originated and lay in music. Another example is to be found in his idea of interconnection. In music, there are no independent elements. How often we think, on a personal, social, or political level, that there are certain independent things and that, upon doing them, will not influence others or that this interconnection will remain hidden! This does not occur in music because in music everything is interconnected. The character and intention of the simplest melody change drastically with a complex harmony. That is learned through music, not through political life. Thus emerges the impossibility of separating elements, the perception that everything is connected, the need to always unite logical thought and intuitive emotion. How often all of us think that we should consider something objectively! We know all too well, but we forget, that emotion will not allow us to do so. How often do we succumb to the temptation of abandoning all logic for the sake of an emotional need, an emotional whim, for the seduction of emotion? In music, this is impossible because music cannot be made exclusively with reason or with emotion. What is more, if those elements may be separated, they are no longer music, but a collection of sounds. If the listener, upon hearing something, can affirm that "it has an impressive logic, but emotionally it wasn't convincing," or, in contrast, "How appealing I found it, what an exciting emotive force it has, though it wasn't very logical," for me, this is no longer music. It wasn't for Said, either.

His concept of inclusion as opposed to exclusion also derived from music, as well as the integration principle, applicable to all sorts of problems. The same could be applied to the discussion of his book *Orientalism*. It speaks of the idea of Oriental seduction versus Western production. In music, there is no production without seduction. There is seduction without production, but not production without seduction. Productive as a musical idea may be, if it is lacking the seduction of the necessary sound, it is insufficient. This is why I say that Edward Said was, for many, a great thinker, a fighter for the rights of his people, and an incomparable intellectual. But for me, he was always, really, a musician, in the deepest sense of the term.

For me, personally, the loss of Edward Said has been a terrible blow because it affects me in so many different areas. His friendship represented an intellectual stimulation such as I have never had and that I will surely never have again, a deep friendship such as I have only rarely experienced, the possibility to share so many serious and banal pleasures and, not so much as gastronomy, to smoke cigars. In so many different ways, since the loss of Said, I feel much poorer than I would like to feel and imagine.

The Palestinian people lost, with his death, one of their most lucid advocates, although he was and is much criticized in his own country. For Israel he was a formidable adversary, although he called for mutual recognition and acceptance of the other's suffering. Yet how many Israeli leaders would have wanted to forget the existence of Edward Said!

Name and Title Index

Includes only titles of works by Edward Said cited in this volume.